Keeping Unusual Pets

Rats

June McNicholas

Raintree

www.raintreepublishers.co.uk
Visit our website to find out more information about Raintree books.

To order:
☎ Phone 0845 6044371
🖷 Fax +44 (0) 1865 312263
✉ Email myorders@capstonepub.co.uk

Customers from outside the UK please telephone +44 1865 312262

Raintree is an imprint of Capstone Global Library Limited, a company incorporated in England and Wales having its registered office at 7 Pilgrim Street, London, EC4V 6LB – Registered company number: 6695582

"Raintree" is a registered trademark of Pearson Education Limited, under licence to Capstone Global Library Limited

Text © Capstone Global Library Limited 2002, 2010
First published in hardback in 2002
2nd edition first published in hardback and paperback in 2010

Edited by Louise Galpine, Megan Cotugno, and Laura Knowles
Designed by Kim Miracle and Ryan Frieson
Picture research by Mica Brancic
Originated by Capstone Global Library Ltd 2010
Printed and bound in China by Leo Paper Products Ltd

ISBN 978 0 431125 54 1 (hardback)
14 13 12 11 10
10 9 8 7 6 5 4 3 2 1

ISBN 978 0 431125 65 7 (paperback)
14 13 12 11 10
10 9 8 7 6 5 4 3 2 1

British Library Cataloguing in Publication Data
McNicholas, June
   Rats. -- 2nd ed. -- (Keeping unusual pets)
636.9'352-dc22
A full catalogue record for this book is available from the British Library.

Acknowledgements
We would like to thank the following for permission to reproduce photographs: Ardea p. **20 bottom** (Johann de Meester); Bruce Coleman Collection pp. **7 top** (© Jane Burton), **42** (© Andrew Percell); © Capstone Global Library Ltd pp. **5, 8 top, 8 bottom, 9 top, 9 bottom, 11 top, 12, 14, 18 bottom, 19, 20 top, 22, 23 left, 23 right, 24, 25 bottom, 25 top, 26 left, 26 right, 27, 29 left, 29 right, 31 top, 31 bottom, 33, 35 top, 35 bottom, 37 top, 40** (Gareth Boden Photography), **43** (Maria Joannou), **16, 30, 34, 36, 37 bottom, 38, 41, 45 top, 45 bottom** (Tudor Photography); © Capstone Publishers pp. **15, 17, 18 top, 21, 28, 32 left, 32 right** (Karon Dubke); iStockphoto pp. **44 top** (© Alexander Novikov), **44 bottom** (© Dmitry Maslov); NHPA pp. **7** (© Stephen Dalton), **39** (© Daniel Heuclin); Science Photo Library pp. **5, 11, 13**; Shutterstock pp. **6** (krechet), **11 bottom** (Ragnarock).

Cover photograph of a rat reproduced with permission of Shutterstock (© Pakhnyushcha).

We would like to thank Judy Tuma and Rob Lee for their invaluable help in the preparation of this book.

Every effort has been made to contact copyright holders of material reproduced in this book. Any omissions will be rectified in subsequent printings if notice is given to the publishers.

Disclaimer
All the Internet addresses (URLs) given in this book were valid at the time of going to press. However, due to the dynamic nature of the Internet, some addresses may have changed, or sites may have changed or ceased to exist since publication. While the author and Publishers regret any inconvenience this may cause readers, no responsibility for any such changes can be accepted by either the author or the Publishers.

No animals were harmed during the process of taking photographs for this series.

Contents

Any words appearing in the text in bold, **like this**, are explained in the glossary.

What is a rat?

Most people think of rats as nasty wild animals that live in sewers and spread diseases. So do not be surprised if people ask you how you could possibly want to keep a rat as a pet!

But are pet rats really so horrible? The answer is, not a bit! Pet rats are not the same as wild rats that **scavenge**, or hunt for food, in rubbish tips or sewers. They have been **domesticated** for many years so they now make excellent and friendly pets.

Many people think that rats are the best small pets for adults and children.

From the wild to our homes

Several centuries ago, people known as rat catchers were paid to kill **pest** rats. Eventually they started keeping unusually coloured rats and began **breeding** them. This was the beginning of the many colour varieties of today's pet rats. In 1901, a lady asked if she could exhibit her pet rats at a show in England. Her black and white rat won "Best of Show." Since then, rats have become popular pets. A wild rat's lifespan is about one year, but domestic rats live for two to three years. This is because they are raised with good food, fresh water, and receive medical care.

FAMOUS RATS

One of the most famous pet rats was a white rat called Sammy. Sammy belonged to Beatrix Potter, the author of the Peter Rabbit stories.

Wild rats often live on rubbish tips. They survive by eating anything they can find.

NEED TO KNOW

✪ Wild rats are classed as **vermin**, or pests. It is **illegal** to keep vermin so you must not take rats from the wild.

✪ Domesticated rats should not be allowed to breed with wild rats or be released into the wild.

✪ Children are not allowed to buy pets themselves. You should learn about pet rats and their care from a **breeder**, someone who already has a rat, reference books, and the internet. Your family must agree on bringing a new pet into your home.

✪ Most countries have laws protecting animals. It is your responsibility to make sure your rats are healthy and well cared for. Always take your pets to the vet if they are ill or have been injured.

Rat facts

Rats are **mammals**. This means they are **warm-blooded** creatures (they produce their own body heat) which give birth to their young and feed their babies with their milk. They are members of the **rodent** family, which includes mice, rabbits, guinea pigs, gerbils, and hamsters. In fact, quite a lot of small pets are rodents!

All rodents have long teeth for gnawing. A rat's teeth grow throughout its life so rats need to gnaw to keep their teeth short. If their teeth grow too long, they can die of starvation because they cannot eat properly.

Rats are members of the rodent family. Like all rodents, they will gnaw on things to keep their teeth short.

DID YOU KNOW?

- ✪ Rats live for around two to three years.
- ✪ Male rats are called **bucks**.
- ✪ Female rats are called **does**.
- ✪ The longest life span for a domestic rat was seven years and four months.
- ✪ There are rats that do not have fur. Those rats must be protected from extreme temperatures.
- ✪ France launched an astronaut rat into outer space in 1961.
- ✪ A rat's tail may be as long as its body.

Rat babies

Rats **mature**, or grow up, very quickly and can have babies of their own when they are only two or three months old. This is one reason why rats can be such **pests** in the wild. Rats have lots of babies in a **litter**. They can have several litters in a year, by which time the babies will have grown up enough to have babies of their own!

Clever climbers

Rats are fast-moving, **agile** creatures that are good at climbing. They are very intelligent and are good at solving problems! You can teach a rat to run through a maze to its food and it will remember which route is the quickest! Their intelligence is another reason why rats are pests in the wild – they can find food easily and can escape from humans and their traps – but it is also what makes rats very good pets.

Baby rats are called **kittens** or pups. When they are first born, they have no hair on their bodies and they cannot see.

Rats use their long tails to help them keep their balance.

Different colours

Pet rats come in lots of different colours. Colours for rats include white, cinnamon (reddish-brown), champagne (cream), chocolate (dark brown), and blue (smoky grey-blue). Rats of specific colours are grouped into types and are often called **fancy rats**. There are also rats that do not belong to a particular type, but they still look pretty and make good pets.

This picture shows a chocolate hooded rat (left) and a champagne hooded rat (right).

These rats are a silverthorn (left) and a chocolate rat (right).

A wide choice

There are lots of different types of fancy rat to choose from! A good way to find out more about these varieties is to get in touch with a rat society – you can find details of these at the end of this book. You could also contact your local rat club, visit some rat shows, or talk to rat owners. You will soon find out that rats make excellent pets and discover that they are nothing like their wild cousins.

The rat above is a mink variegated rat.

This picture shows a Berkshire rat (top) and a hooded rat (bottom).

Are rats for you?

Some people may tell you that rats make the best small pets of all because they are so intelligent and friendly. They might even think that they are more fun to keep than cats or dogs.

As with all pets, there are good and bad things about owning rats. Here are some of the good points and not-so-good points.

GOOD POINTS

- ✪ Rats are intelligent. They recognize their owners and love human company.

- ✪ Rats will quickly learn your routine. You may find them waiting at the front of their cage when it is time for them to be taken out!

- ✪ Rats are not truly **nocturnal**, so they are happy to be up and active when you are.

- ✪ Rats are not expensive to buy or to feed.

- ✪ Above all, rats have character. They have big personalities in small bodies. This makes them real friends – some are more like little dogs or cats!

NOT-SO-GOOD POINTS

- ✪ A rat can bite hard if it is hurt or frightened.

- ✪ Rats will chew absolutely anything they can reach from their cage.

- ✪ Some **bucks** like to mark places where they have been with a few drops of **urine**. This does not smell, but it can be off-putting for some people.

- ✪ Sadly, rats do not live long. Most of them only live for about 24 to 30 months.

Yes or no?

So, are rats for you? Having rats for pets means giving them food and water every day, cleaning out their cage every week, and playing with them for about one hour every day. Are you really sure that you are prepared to do all these things, even when you are in a hurry or want to do something else? If the answer is yes, then you could be ready to begin keeping rats as pets. This hobby could last for many years – or even for the rest of your life!

Your rats will love to sit on your shoulder. They will probably play with your hair and might even lick your face!

When your rats see you coming, they will run to the front of their cage – all ready to play with you!

11

Choosing your rats

There are lots of things to think about when you are choosing a rat. Always take an adult with you to help you choose your pet, and if possible ask an experienced rat keeper to come along too and give you advice.

One or more?

Rats like the company of other rats. It is not exactly wrong to keep a single rat, but you will have to give your pet a lot of time and attention. A lone rat will probably be very unhappy.

It is much better to keep two rats rather than one. They will be just as friendly with you, but they will also have each other for company when you are busy. In fact, two rats will be twice the fun! Try to choose two rats of the same age who are already used to each other. Best of all, choose two sisters or two brothers.

Rats are naturally **gregarious**. They enjoy playing with other rats.

Buck or doe?

Usually, **bucks** are bigger than **does**. Bucks are also lazier, so they are probably the best choice if you want a pet that will sit quietly on your lap. The one drawback with bucks is that some of them like to mark the places they have been with a few drops of **urine**. This is a scent mark to let other rats know that your rat is around. We cannot smell it but other rats can. It is less of a problem than it sounds, but some people do not like the idea very much.

TOP TIPS

✪ If you decide to keep more than one rat, make sure that all your rats are the same sex. If they are not, you could end up with far more pets than you had planned for!

✪ Both bucks and does make equally good pets, so the choice is up to you.

✪ Try to visit some rat keepers and rat shows to get to know a few bucks and does before you decide which will suit you best.

Does are usually more lively and playful than bucks. Most does do not mark places with urine, but a few of them (usually the very bossy ones!) do it just as much as bucks.

If you have two rats, they will keep each other company when you are not around.

What age?

It is best to choose pet rats of about eight weeks old. Older rats take longer to get used to their human owners and rats under six weeks are too young to leave their mothers. Unfortunately, many pet shop owners will not know exactly how old their rats are, or even what sex they are. However, if you take an experienced rat keeper with you to help select your rats, they may be able to help.

These young rats look healthy and **alert**, with bright eyes and shiny coats. They would make excellent pets.

TOP TIP

Never buy a rat if it seems unwell or if its nose, eyes, ears, or rear end are not clean and free of discharge.

What to look for

There are a few basic things to look out for when you are choosing rats.

- ✪ The rats should be living in clean surroundings.
- ✪ They should be young, have bright eyes, a clean nose, mouth, ears, and tail.
- ✪ Their coats should be soft and clean, with no sores or bald patches.
- ✪ They should be interested in you, and settle down quickly when you hold them.

TOP TIP

If you are choosing a doe, make sure she has been separated from male rats since she was eight weeks old. Otherwise, she could be pregnant. It is unfair for an animal so young to **breed** when she is no more than a baby herself and still has a lot of growing up to do.

Your local rat **breeder** should have plenty of rats to choose from. Take a little time to get to know the rats before you choose any.

What do I need?

Rats can be kept in cages or tanks, but the most important thing is to give your pets plenty of room. Rats are active and playful creatures and they will make good use of whatever space you provide.

Choosing a cage

Most people keep their pet rats in a cage. A cage measuring about 60 × 40 × 40 centimetres (24 x 16 x 16 inches) is about right for a pair of rats, but get a bigger one if you can.

Many pet shops stock cages especially for rats. Look for one that is roomy and easy to clean. Cages with metal bars and plastic trays in their base are simple to keep clean. Doors and cage panels need to be secure enough to prevent the rat from escaping, so test them carefully before you buy your cage.

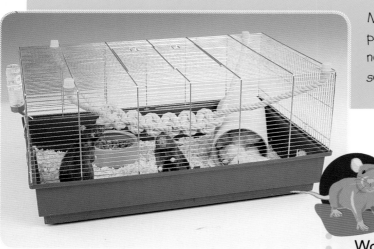

Most cages have metal bars and a plastic base. Make sure the bars are narrow enough to stop a rat from squeezing through!

TOP TIP

Wooden cages are not ideal. Rats will eventually gnaw them to pieces. They are difficult to keep clean as **urine** soaks into the wood, causing it to smell and rot.

Choosing a tank

Another way of keeping rats is in a glass tank. However, it is very important to find a suitable lid for the tank. Choose one that lets in air but does not have large enough holes for your rats to climb through! It is very important to let enough air into the tank because otherwise **condensation** (drops of water) can collect on the inside of the tank walls, making it damp. This can be dangerous to a rat's health.

TOP TIP

Rats love to climb, so choose a cage that is tall enough to fit ramps, ladders, ropes, or branches inside so that your rats can exercise and play.

There is plenty of space in this cage for climbing toys to keep your rats busy.

The perfect place

Once you have chosen your pets' home, you will need to find the right place for it. Rats can suffer from **heatstroke** if the temperature rises above 24°Celsius (75°Fahrenheit), so keep the cage out of direct sunlight and away from hot radiators. Rats can also become ill if the temperature drops below 7°C (45°F) or if they are kept in a draught. Choose a sheltered place for their cage where they will not be too hot or too cold, and where there is not much variation in temperature.

Keep your cage on a table or shelf where the rats will not be bothered by other family pets.

Wood shavings

You will need something to cover the floor of your rats' cage. Wood shavings are best. Make sure that you buy them from good pet shops rather than direct from a timber yard. You do not want your wood shavings to be full of nails, splinters, tea bags, and other assorted rubbish! More seriously, wood shavings from timber yards may contain germs from wild rats and mice that could make your pet rats ill.

The wood shavings should not be too fine or dusty, or they may hurt a rat's eyes or get up its nose.

Bedding

Rats need material to make themselves a bed. You can use shredded paper for bedding, but avoid newspaper as the ink is not good for rats. Paper towels are fine – let the rats do the tearing up! Straw and hay are not suitable because they are not absorbent and do not get rid of smells.

TOP TIP

If good wood shavings are hard to find, try using cat litter pellets made from recycled paper. Some rat owners prefer to use these.

Bedding boxes

You may want to make a bedding box for your rats. A terracotta flower pot filled with bedding is fine. So is a cardboard shoebox with a rat-sized hole cut into its side. However, the rats will soon start chewing on the box. A bedding box will give your rats somewhere private to sleep. There are endless possibilities – you will find yourself looking at things and thinking, "I could give that to my rat to sleep in or play with."

Your rats will enjoy their comfortable sleeping box.

Toys for rats

Rats are playful and inquisitive creatures, so toys are a must. Your pets will enjoy having ladders and branches to climb on, shelves to run along, and tunnels to explore. Blocks of untreated and unpainted wood will give your rats something to chew on so they can keep their teeth short. Apple and pear wood are best. You can also buy chewing blocks from your pet shop or rat **breeder**.

Blocks of wood are good for a rat's teeth and provide hours of chewing fun.

Climbing around

Many rat cages are fitted with shelves, ramps, and ladders, but you can also give your pets some branches to climb on. Choose dry, rough branches that are still covered with bark.

NOT TOO FULL!

Do not fill your pets' cage so full of toys that there is not enough room for them to run around! Most of all, rats enjoy plenty of open space.

Rats love climbing through, over, and under things!

Buying and making

Many pet shops and rat breeders sell colourful plastic tunnels, slides, and houses for rats to explore. You can also make your own rat toys from wide cardboard tubes and boxes with holes cut out of them. Try mixing up your pets' plastic toys with things you have made yourself to create an obstacle course. You could even try making a maze for your rats. Rats are so clever that your pets will soon find their way through the maze.

Your rats will have fun with almost anything you give them. But do not let your pets play with something they might swallow.

No wheels

Exercise wheels are not good for rats. They are often too small for adult rats, especially some of the hefty **bucks**. Wheels with open bars can be dangerous as rats' tails can get caught up in the bars and injured. Solid wheels are usually made of plastic so rats will chew at them. Many plastic wheels have nasty metal spikes in the middle which are exposed once the plastic coating is gone. It is much better for your rats to have other toys to play with and to have lots of exercise time outside their cage.

Looking after your rats

Your rat cage will need to be cleaned out thoroughly once a week. Throw out all the wood shavings and bedding and wipe down the cage with a mild disinfectant. You can buy safe cleaning products from a pet shop. Do not forget to wipe down the shelves as well as any toys or branches in the cage. When everything is thoroughly rinsed and completely dry, put in fresh wood shavings and bedding and put all the toys, branches, and shelves back inside the cage.

Rat **urine** can become quite smelly, so you and your family will soon notice if you do not clean the cage regularly!

A weekly clean does not take long and will keep your rats' home smelling sweet.

TOP TIP

You will not need to spend much time keeping your rats clean. Rats are naturally very clean animals and they spend a lot of time **grooming** themselves. However, rats' tails can sometimes get grubby. You can clean them with mild soap and water. Just rub the tail gently with a cloth, then rinse it with clean water.

Bath time

Rats rarely need baths, but they will need one if you decide to enter them for shows. If you treat your rats gently, bath times will not be stressful.

- ✪ Dip your rats into a bowl of lukewarm water and then hold them out of the water while you use a pet-safe shampoo on their coats and tails. Be careful not to let any shampoo get into their eyes or ears.

- ✪ Rinse your pets off in clean warm water and dry them with a towel. Talk softly and soothingly while you are doing this.

- ✪ Make sure your rats are completely dry and comfortable before they return to their cage.

DAILY CLEANING

As well as giving the cage a weekly clean, you will also have some clearing up to do every day.

- ✪ Remove any uneaten food that is left scattered around the cage, especially fruit or vegetables that can attract flies.

- ✪ Wash the food bowl.

- ✪ Check the water bottle to make sure it is clean and fill it with fresh water.

- ✪ Remove any **faeces** scattered about the cage.

- ✪ Scoop out any wood shavings made wet with urine.

- ✪ Rats can have an annoying habit of wetting their beds. Check that your rats' bedding is clean and dry.

Washing is easiest if you have two bowls, side by side – one for washing and the other for rinsing.

After you have dried your rats, they may like to scamper around a bit to get warmed up!

Food for rats

Your rats' basic diet should be a mixture of grains and cereals that you can buy from a pet shop. Rat food is sold in boxes or packets or even loose. However, do make sure that the food is meant for rats. Gerbil and hamster food contains a lot of sunflower seeds and nuts, which rats love, but can cause sore spots on a rat's skin. It is much better to feed your rats a proper rat food, and give them an occasional sunflower seed or nut as a treat. Follow the feeding instructions on the packet as a guideline to how much you should feed your pets.

Only feed your rats food that has been especially prepared for rats.

Healthy extras

You can add a few extra **ingredients** to your rats' basic diet. Wholemeal bread or toast, unsweetened breakfast cereals, cooked rice or noodles, and cooked potato will all be appreciated by your pets – but don't overdo it! Your rats will also enjoy chewing on a dog biscuit – this is a tasty way to keep their teeth healthy.

FRUIT AND VEGETABLES

Washed fruit and vegetables are good for rats. Start by giving your rats small amounts, to see which kinds they prefer.

✪ The best fruits are apples, although some rats love melon, cherries, and peaches! Do not feed your rats very acidic fruits such as oranges.

✪ Carrots, romaine lettuce, cabbage, and celery are good vegetables to give your rats.

✪ Do not feed onions or very strong tasting vegetables to your pets.

Feeding times

You can choose when to feed your rats, but it is usually best to feed them in the evening with a top-up in the morning for breakfast if they need it. Rats will store extra food that they are not hungry enough to eat. Large stores mean that you are overfeeding them!

Most rats love nibbling on fresh fruit and vegetables.

Rats are enthusiastic eaters! They often climb right inside their feeding bowl.

SAFETY FIRST

Rats can get tummy upsets from eating too much fruit or too many vegetables. Stick to very small amounts and only give your rats fruit or vegetables every other day.

Tasty treats

You can buy various treats made especially for rats. These may be bars of cereals to be attached to the cage, tasty yogurt drops, or small biscuits. Rats enjoy these, but you can offer them lots of other things too. Your rats will almost certainly enjoy a small taste of biscuit, chocolate, cake, or even ice-cream – but do not give them too much! You know how bad it is to eat too much of these things, but your rats do not. A tiny taste now and again is okay but it is up to you not to let your rats get fat or ill by eating too many of the wrong foods.

TOP TIP

Normally, if you like eating something, your rats will probably like it too!

Your rats will probably love a small taste of ice cream, but never give them this much!

Pet shops sell a range of healthy treats like this.

A bony treat!

A good tasty treat for rats is a small, cooked bone with a little meat still on it. Rats enjoy meat and chewing on the bone is good for their teeth. Bone can also provide valuable **calcium** which will help your pets to have strong teeth and bones. A clean, cooked bone can be left in the cage for a day or so, but meaty bones must be removed after one day, as they will soon go bad and start to smell.

Rats need to drink lots of water. Remember to fill their bottle with new, fresh water every day.

Water bottles

Finally, and very importantly, rats should always have fresh water to drink. A water bottle hung from the outside of the cage wires is best. You can also buy a clip to hang a water bottle from the lid of a tank. Water bottles work by letting drops of water flow whenever a rat licks the end of the spout. That way, your pets can get enough to drink without their bottle dripping into the cage.

HOLIDAYS

Rats need daily care. If you are going away, make sure you have arranged for someone to look after your pets.

✪ Ask a friend or neighbour who knows and likes rats.

✪ Show the person how much food to give your pets and how to change the water. If you will be gone a long time, show the person how to clean the cage.

✪ You should leave clear written instructions about how much to feed your pets, a phone number to reach you, and the vet's phone number.

Happy and healthy?

You need to check your pets regularly to make sure they are fit and well. Are your rats eating the proper amount and drinking regularly? Do they seem lively and **alert**? When you clean out the cage, check your rats' faeces. They should not be very runny or too hard.

Daily checks

While you are handling your rats, feel them all over to make sure there are no lumps, bumps, or swellings on their bodies. Check that your pets' coats are clean and soft, with no sores or specks of dirt from fleas. Make sure that the skin on their ears and tails is clean and smooth, not rough and scaly.

TOP TIP

If you see something that could be a problem, tell your parents or another adult. They can help you decide whether you need to take your pet to the vet.

Look through each rat's fur to make sure there is no flea dirt.

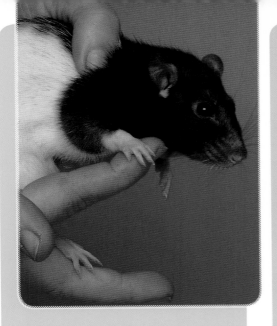

Check your rat's nails. If they are very long they should be trimmed.

This rat's teeth are the correct length. If your rat's teeth are longer than this, you will need to take your pet to the vet to have its teeth clipped.

Sometimes a rat's nails need trimming. Ask your vet to trim the nails to show you how to do it safely. Also, check your pets' teeth. Rats' teeth keep growing all the time and if your pets are not chewing enough, their teeth can become **overgrown**. If a rat's teeth become too long they can even stop it from feeding properly. You can find out more about health problems on pages 36 to 41.

WATCH OUT!

Here are some things to look out for when you are playing with your rats.

✪ Watch how your rats move around. A limp or an unusual way of walking may mean that your rat has been injured or is in pain.

✪ Are your pets getting fatter or thinner? A change in weight can be a sign of a serious health problem.

✪ Is one of your rats holding its head on one side? This may mean it has an ear problem.

Handling your rats

Pet rats are not wild animals. They have been **domesticated** so they are happy to live with people. But this does not mean you will be able to handle your rats immediately. As with every friendship, human or animal, it will take a little time to get to know each other and feel confident together.

A new home

When you first take your rats home, give them time to settle in before you try to play with them or handle them.

Some rats settle in quicker than others. Some will be standing up at the bars demanding your attention as soon as they have explored their cage. Others will be quite shy and will have to be coaxed out of their cage. Food is always a great way of making friends! Quietly offer a tasty titbit and let the rat take it from your fingers. If you have a very shy rat, you may need to put a titbit near the front of the cage and sit quietly while it plucks up the courage to take it.

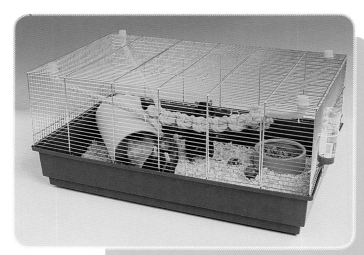

Your rats will probably take a while to explore their new home and settle in comfortably.

TOP TIP

Do not try to pick up your pets straight away. Remember that your hand will look enormous to a rat, so it has to learn that you will not hurt it.

Slowly does it

Take some time to allow your rats to get used to your voice and your hands. Your pets will have had a lot of changes in their short lives and they will need to feel confident. Soon they will be taking food from you – first through the bars of their cage and then directly from your hand. They may even start putting their little feet on the palm of your hand while they take their food. This sort of confidence means that a rat is ready to be handled.

You will seem like a giant to your rats! Talk to them softly and let them get used to the sound of your voice.

OTHER PETS

✪ You will need to be very careful about letting your rats meet other pets. Cats and dogs have the natural **instinct** to kill rats. Take care when you introduce them and never leave them alone together.

✪ Rats can also badly frighten or even kill some other pets. Do not let them near hamsters or gerbils, even if they are in their cages. It may be too upsetting for the smaller animal.

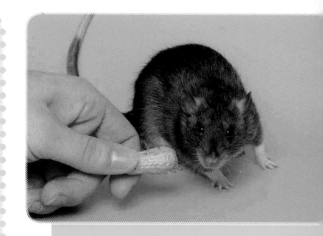

Your rats will soon be happy to take a titbit from your fingers.

Picking up your rat

Never pick up a rat by its tail. This is very frightening for your pet and may even injure it. Pick up a rat by putting one hand over its back and scooping it up into your other hand. This means that it will be sitting on one of your hands with your other hand over it. Stroke it and speak softly to it and try not to do anything too suddenly.

At first, a rat may not seem to like being handled, but it is important to hold it as much as you can so that it gets used to being held. Remember to always hold your rat with both hands. You need to be careful to stop him or her accidentally falling or jumping.

Offer a treat, such as a little bit of ice cream on your fingers. Your pet will soon learn that handling means nice things are going to happen!

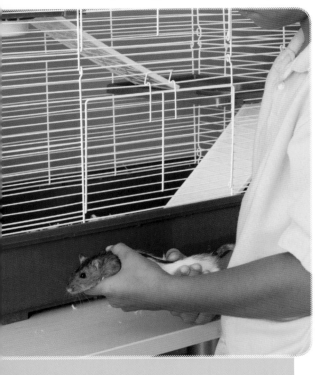

Be firm, gentle, and confident when you pick up your rat.

A rat will like being held against your body while you support its bottom with your other hand.

Contented chuckles

As your rats become more confident, let them sit on your shoulder. This is a favourite place for many rats, and they will happily sit with you while you watch TV or walk around the house. Often a happy rat will "chuckle" and make a tooth-grinding noise which can sound quite loud when it is right in your ear! Some rats even lick their owner's face. They have very soft, velvety tongues and very tickly whiskers!

TOP TIP

If your rats try to hide in your clothing – let them! Rats love being carried around in their owner's jumper or T-shirt, so it can be a good way of getting your pets used to riding around on you.

Playtime

You should spend some time every day playing with your rats outside of their cage. It is best to keep your rats in just one or two rooms where you can stay with them and make sure that they do not get into any trouble. You can give your pets some tubes and boxes to play in, but they will mainly enjoy just being out and exploring.

TOP TIP

You should always remember to wash your hands after handling a rat.

Your rat will love the new sights and scents outside of its cage.

Rat-proofing a room

Before you let your rats out to play, you will need to make sure that they cannot get hurt. You will also have to keep things safe from your rats! Be careful that there is nothing in their reach that they can chew to bits.

Inspect the room for any places where a rat could get stuck or lost. The best way to do this is to pretend to be a rat! Lie down flat on the floor and ask yourself what you can see that is rat-sized and might seem worth exploring. Look for gaps in walls, fireplaces, behind cupboards, or cracks in floorboards and under doors. These will all need blocking up. Check also that your pets cannot get inside furniture. A number of pet rats meet a sudden death by being sat on in sofas or chairs.

Before you let your rats out to play, make sure you cover any electric cables.

Electricity alert

Rats love chewing things. Electric cables and TV, video, and computer leads all look like tasty things for a rat to chew on. This could be very dangerous for your pet because it might get an electric shock that could kill it. If there are some cables that cannot be moved, fit protective cable sleeves round them to stop them from being chewed.

Chewing trouble

Rats can be quite destructive if you are not careful. A favourite trick is to chew any material they can reach from their cage. Do not put clothing, papers, or other items near your pets' cage. They may reach out and drag them in! And if a rat disappears behind the curtains when it is out playing, it may well be chewing holes in them!

If you leave anything close to your pets' cage, your rats will try to find a way of dragging it inside!

Rats take a fancy to objects that they can pick up and carry. Key rings, sweet wrappers, pens, and even jewellery may all find their way into a rat's hiding place!

TOP TIPS

✪ Rats often steal things. This can be amusing but rats are not clever enough to know when something is really harmful.

✪ Check your room to see what is lying around and remove any precious objects or things that would be bad for your rats to chew on.

Some health problems

Rats are quite healthy little animals but there are a few illnesses and problems that rat owners need to recognize. Because rats are very small, they can get ill very fast – so having an experienced vet nearby is important.

Colds

Runny eyes and nose, wheezing, and sneezing may well mean that your rat has a cold. Rats can catch colds if they are in a draught, if the temperature drops dramatically, or if they are near another rat with a cold. Sometimes the liquid from your rat's eyes and nose may be pink and look like blood, but it is not. Colds can be quite serious to rats, so take your pet to the vet. The vet may give your pet **medicine** to help fight the cold. You must also keep it away from other rats to stop them catching the cold too. Make sure your rat is warm, drinking lots of water, and eating normally.

If your rat becomes seriously ill, take it straight to the vet.

Skin problems

Spots and sores on a rat's skin can be painful and itchy. There are two main causes of skin problems in rats. The first is diet. Your rat may have been eating too many sunflower seeds or nuts. If this is the case, replace its normal diet with very simple food for a few days, such as boiled rice and plain bread. If your rat's skin starts to look better, then diet was probably the cause.

The second cause of sores, scabs, and bald patches are **mites**. These are tiny **parasites** that live in some animals' coats. They may have come from hay or straw that they were in before you got them, or from another rat. If you have recently bought a new rat, you should ask your vet to check it for mites. If your pet has mites, your vet will give you a special shampoo to kill the mites. Change all the bedding and wood shavings in your pet's cage and do not let it near other rats until it is clear of mites.

TUMMY TROUBLES

- **Diarrhoea** is often caused by too many fruits and vegetables or by too many unhealthy treats. This is easily put right. Just feed your rat a very plain diet for a few days.

- Sometimes, a rat can develop diarrhoea if it is stressed from travelling or being moved from place to place. This normally settles down on its own.

- If your rat is suffering from **constipation** it will have very hard **faeces** that are difficult to pass. Constipation can be very painful. It is often caused by too much dried food. Feeding your rat with a little lettuce or salad greens can improve things.

Normal rat faeces should be quite soft and **cylindrical** in shape. If they are runny or very dry, your rat has a problem.

Ear problems

If your rat starts to hold its head tilted to one side there is probably something wrong with its ears. Your rat may even have trouble balancing. Your vet will give you some ear drops to help clear the **infection**. Rats usually recover with a week or two of treatments.

Lumps and bumps

Many rats develop lumps and bumps. Sometimes these may be soft and full of **pus**. These are called **abscesses** and are caused by an infection developing around a wound or a bite. Abscesses can be drained and cleaned and usually heal up very well.

Your vet will be able to give you advice about what to look for when examining your rats.

Other lumps may be firmer. Most of these lumps are **benign**, which means they are harmless. They can often be removed by an operation. Sadly, rats sometimes develop **cancerous tumours**. These often feel just like the benign lumps, but they grow fast and eventually make the rat very ill. If this happens, you should talk to your vet about whether it would be best to have your rat **put down**.

Teeth problems

A rat's teeth keep on growing throughout its life, so your pets will need lots of hard things to gnaw on to wear down their teeth. Sometimes, a rat's teeth can grow so long that it cannot eat properly and starts to lose weight. If this happens, your vet can clip your rat's teeth to the right length. Your rat will not like it, but it will not hurt.

A rat's teeth keep growing all the time. This rat has lost one of its upper teeth so its lower tooth has not worn down and has grown extremely long.

TOP TIP

Make sure you give your pets lots of hard blocks of wood and other things to chew on to keep their teeth the right length.

EYE PROBLEMS

✪ If your rat has watery or runny eyes, ask an adult to help you bathe them with a soft tissue soaked in warm water. There may just be a speck of dust in your rat's eye.

✪ If the trouble comes back after bathing the eyes, it could be an infection. You will need to take your rat to the vet for some **medicine**.

Too hot

If your rats' cage is left in direct sunlight or too close to a hot radiator, your pets will become overheated and suffer from **heatstroke**. They will look uncomfortable and distressed and their breathing will become rapid and shallow. Quickly move the cage to cooler surroundings and encourage your rats to drink cool water. If your rats collapse, wrap them in cool (not ice cold) damp towels and take them to the vet.

Too cold

If your rats become really cold, they may suffer from **hypothermia**. They will seem very slow and sluggish and may even collapse. Their bodies will be hunched up and feel cold to the touch. The best thing to do is to pop your pets inside your shirt so your body temperature heats them up gently. If your rats do not show signs of getting better in ten minutes, take them to the vet straight away.

TOP TIP

If a rat becomes too cold, a little drink of warm milk or water will help to increase its body temperature.

If one of your rats develops hypothermia, you need to act fast. You could try taking it to a warm place and wrapping it up in a towel or blanket.

DANGER SIGNS

Watch out for these danger signs. They might mean that one of your rats is very ill.

✪ Your rat is sitting hunched up as if it is very uncomfortable. Its eyes may be half closed or it may be trembling. Its coat may look scruffy because it is not **grooming** itself.

✪ Your rat cannot walk without falling over. It may have a severe ear infection.

✪ Your rat has difficulty breathing, and is gasping and wheezing. This may mean that the rat has **pneumonia**.

If your rat has any of these signs, you should contact your vet immediately.

If your rat is looking more scruffy than normal, it may be a sign that your pet is unwell.

Accidents can happen

Sometimes rats get broken legs. If this happens, you will need to take your pet to a vet very quickly. The vet will decide whether an operation is necessary to help mend the leg. Sometimes it may be necessary to **amputate** (cut off) a leg. Rats cope surprisingly well with only three legs. Occasionally a rat may have to be put down if its injuries are very serious.

In spite of these possible illnesses, you will probably find that your rats are healthy and active little creatures for most of their lives. However, a rat's life is short – only about two and a half years – so it will not be long before you have to think about your rat as an old animal.

Growing old

Old rats need special care. They feel the cold more and are less active and **agile** than younger rats. It is a good idea to remove any ladders and climbing toys from their cage, as their balance may not be very good.

Give an old rat a quiet life with lots of gentle care and affection. It will still have a lot to enjoy even if it is not as lively as it used to be. Even though it is old and slow, your rat will still be a friend who likes to sit on your shoulder.

Once a rat is over two years old, it will probably start to look old.

A peaceful end

Some old rats die peacefully in their sleep without ever becoming really ill. Others get lots of little illnesses, aches, and pains. These can mean that an old rat's life is no longer very enjoyable.

If your rat is old and sick and near the end of its life, you may decide that it is a good idea to talk to your vet about having it **put down**. The injection does not hurt, it just makes your pet feel sleepy. Before you can count to ten, your rat's heart will beat for the last time.

SAYING GOODBYE

It is hard to lose a pet that you have loved. It can seem very unfair that your rat has lived for such a short time. However, there are some things that you need to remember.

✪ It is not your fault, or the vet's fault, that your pet has died. It is just a hard fact that rats do not live long.

✪ When a pet dies, it is perfectly normal for people, adults as well as children, to cry for a while.

✪ Eventually the pain will pass and you will be left with happy memories of your pet. Maybe you will soon think about having another rat to look after and enjoy?

It can help to have a special burial place for your pet and to plant a flower or a shrub on it.

Keeping a record

It is fun to keep a record of your pet rats. Buy a big scrapbook and fill it with notes and photos. Then you can look back at it and remind yourself of all the things you and your pets did together. Your rat scrapbook can also include general information about rats and how to care for them.

A special diary

Of course, pride of place in your scrapbook will go to your own rats. You could start with the very first photo taken of them when they came to live with you. Were they really those tiny **kittens**? Or what about the first time you held them? Or when they first sat on your shoulder? Or when Mum or Grandma were brave enough to hold them?

You can note down special events in the lives of your pets, such as the first time they explored your room or learned a clever trick. You can also make a note of the funny things your rats do when they are eating or playing.

Choosing which pictures to put in your scrapbook can be a lot of fun. Maybe you could ask other people which ones they like best too.

Useful information

You can collect articles and information about rats and rat care and stick them into your scrapbook. They will soon build up into a good store of tips and guidance. You can also keep lists of your friends and contacts in rat clubs, the dates of shows, and useful websites about rats and how to look after them.

Rat shows

You may decide to show your rats. Societies such as the National Fancy Rat Society in the UK and the Australian Rat Fanciers Society in Australia have junior memberships and junior classes at shows. Maybe your rats will win rosettes that you can keep in your scrapbook!

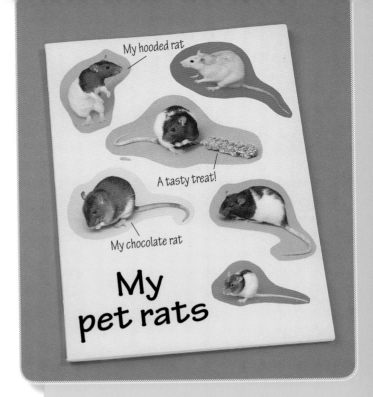

My hooded rat

A tasty treat!

My chocolate rat

My pet rats

When you have finished adding pictures to your scrapbook, it may be a good idea to label them. Otherwise, in years to come, you may forget what each picture is showing.

Your scrapbook should help to make sure that you never forget the special times that you and your rats enjoyed together.

Glossary

abscess soft lump filled with pus

agile able to move quickly and easily

alert lively and interested in everything

amputate cut off a leg or an arm

benign harmless or not dangerous

breed mate and produce young

breeder person who keeps animals to produce young

buck male rat

calcium substance that is good for building strong teeth and bones

cancerous caused by cancer. Cancer is a disease that destroys the body's healthy cells.

condensation water that collects as drops on a cold surface

constipation problem caused by hard faeces (poo) that makes it difficult to go to the toilet

cylindrical shaped like a tube

diarrhoea runny faeces (poo)

doe female rat

domesticate to tame an animal, so that it can live with people

faeces solid waste matter (poo) passed out of the body

fancy rats rats with special markings or colours, recognized as a particular type by rat societies

gregarious sociable, or fond of company

groom to clean an animal's coat; animals often groom themselves

heatstroke illness caused by getting too hot

hypothermia illness caused by getting too cold

illegal against the law

infection illness caused by germs

instinct natural tendency

ingredient part of a food or meal

kitten baby rat

litter group of baby rats born together

mammal animal with fur or hair on its body that feeds its babies with milk

mature to become adult

medicine substance used to treat illnesses

mite small creature that lives on another animal's skin and sucks its blood

nocturnal active at night

overgrown grown too long

parasites small creatures such as fleas or worms that live on or inside another animal

pest creature that causes problems for people, often by carrying diseases

pneumonia illness where the lungs become infected and fill with fluid

pus thick yellow fluid inside an infected part of the body

put down give a sick animal an injection to help it die peacefully and without pain

rodent animal with strong front teeth for gnawing

scavenge hunt for food

tumour lump or growth

urine liquid passed out of the body containing water and waste substances

vermin animals that are pests, such as wild rats and mice

warm-blooded used to describe an animal that can keep its body at the same temperature

Find out more

Books

There are not many books about rats written for young readers. Most of these books are not specially written for children but can be enjoyed by rat owners of all ages:

Rat Training: A Comprehensive Beginner's Guide, Miriam Fields-Babineau (BowTie Press, 2009)

Rats, Julie R. Mancini (TFH Publications, 2009)

The Complete Guide to Rat Training, Debbie Docommun (TFH Publications, 2008)

The Wild Side of Pets: Mice and Rats, Jo Waters (Raintree, 2006)

Websites

www.nfrs.org
This is the website for the National Fancy Rat Society. The society can provide you with lots of information about rats and how to care for them. They also have a calendar of rat shows throughout the country.

www.fancy-rats.co.uk
This website has lots of useful information on looking after your pet rat.

www.petalia.com.au/small_pets
You can find lots of information on keeping small animals on this Australian website. Search for "Rats" to find specific information on these friendly pets.

Index

i love knitting

i love knitting

25 LOOPY PROJECTS THAT WILL SHOW YOU HOW TO KNIT EASILY AND QUICKLY

RACHEL HENDERSON

PHOTOGRAPHY BY KATE WHITAKER

KYLE CATHIE LTD

First published in Great Britain in 2006 by
Kyle Cathie Limited
122 Arlington Road
London NW1 7HP
general.enquiries@kyle-cathie.com
www.kylecathie.com

ISBN: 978 1 85626 684 0
10 9 8 7 6 5 4 3

Text © 2006 Rachel Henderson
Design © 2006 Kyle Cathie Ltd
Photography © 2006 Kate Whitaker
Artwork © 2006 Roberta Boyce

Editorial director Muna Reyal
Art direction and design by Jenny Semple
Photography by Kate Whitaker
Styling by Penny Markham
Artwork by Roberta Boyce
Pattern checking by Penny Hill
Copyediting by Kate Haxell
Production: Sha Huxtable and Alice Holloway
Models: Amy Redmond, Jacob Love, Laura Wheatley, Jenny Wheatley

Rachel Henderson is hereby identified as the author of this work in accordance with Section 77 of the Copyright,
Designs and Patents Act 1988.

A Cataloguing in Publication record for this title is available from the British Library.

Colour reproduction by Sang Choy
Printed in Singapore by Star Standard

contents

my knitted world

My story is different. People tend to expect me to say 'Yeah… I've been knitting since I was five years old', but actually it wasn't until I was in my final year of my textile degree that I got the knitting vibe, and a rather addictive strain at that.

I'll always remember my first visit to my local haberdashery. There I was, a typical art student and a wool virgin, getting as excited about the yarn and patterns as I had been about buying my favourite indie band's new album – how could this be? It was then that I realised I was a knitaholic and my obsession with knitting has grown ever since.

going doolally

But when I first started out, I found myself, like many other beginners, driven to distraction by the jargon used in knitting patterns. Now I'm a consultant in hand knitting and I still hear the words, 'it's like a foreign language' muttered by beginner knitters as they dive into their first pattern, their eagerness soon clouded over, quashed by the liberal use of knitting slang. So this book is as jargon-free as I can make it.

Patience is the key, my grandmother used to say when I manically chucked her thin needles and skinny 2-ply yarn in the air, eager to learn the basics, but frustrated at how fiddly it seemed. Patience is something that is becoming more and more unfamiliar as our lives get busier, and sitting down to create something seems almost impossible. But I want to change this.

I want to show you that anyone can knit. That you can knit anywhere (have a look at my extreme knitting photos). And that you can knit something that you might actually want to wear. Or give to somebody. I want to bring out the designer in you. And when you need a break from those noisy needles, I will also show you a few other things you can do with your needles and wool.

customising designs

Once you have mastered the techniques chapter, got yourself a good tension and followed a few of my patterns without getting too tied up in knots, I want you to have a go at my inspirational chapter, 'Customising Designs'. At my knitting circle I'm constantly seeing young girls coming up with their own knitted

designs, so in order to inspire you, I briefed five of my creative friends to come up with a design based on their skills and background. Whether you try Amy's felted flower, Di`s knitted pants, Louise's funky cuff, Suzie's evening bag or Kate's painted bag, I'm hoping that after having a bash at one or two of these projects you will be inspired enough to create your very own knitted designs.

Knitting is such a versatile craft, and customising it is a great way to awaken your creative soul. By changing yarn, adding beads or embroidering, you can create a one-off piece that is personal to you. That's also why I haven't specified specific colours for each project – I want to bring out the designer in you and choosing the colour combinations you like is a great way to start.

When I was working on projects at art college, I remember being so excited to see the end results, and to discuss with each other what our inspiration was and how we got there. Each person's design always differed, whether through colour, shape or the materials they used, or what they were inspired by. Their personalities and favourite skills were literally woven into their projects.

That's what made this book great to work on – it made me feel like a student again. I had almost forgotten how much fun it used to be and I want to pass this excitement onto you.

So I hope that this chapter, Customising Designs, along with the rest of the book, will give you the confidence to start designing. Just pick out some colours and yarns and create your own patterns. Anyone can be a designer and the possibilities are endless. If they can do it, you can too!

knitting and nattering

Nowadays knitting is seen as a 'cool' thing to do, a good way of filling time, whether you're in the pub, in front of the TV or sitting on a train. It is also really sociable and portable – more and more people just take their needles wherever they go, letting their hands work on while they chat to their friends, watch a film or just let their mind relax and wander.

Knitting is great! And that comes straight from the horse's mouth!

After my first book *Pub Knitting*, I wanted to use the same light-hearted approach to knitting. I have come up with fun designs that I hope you will be able to follow without tying yourself up in knots. They won't take too long to knit nor use lots of yarn or complicated techniques, so I hope that you will have lots of fun with it.

This book is called *I Love Knitting* because that's why I wrote it, and that's the way it should be…

Rachel x

how to knit

I'll begin this section by saying that knitting is easier than it looks, even if you're not a naturally creative person and you think that you have big clumsy hands. All those fiddly-looking techniques often put people off, but if you treat learning to knit like any other skill you've embarked on in the past, you'll find that once you've grasped the basics anything is possible and after a few months you will no doubt be addicted!

What you will need
(p15)

Super chunky wool | Soft chunky wool with ribbon | Supersoft tweed aran mix | Chunky textured wool

getting started

There is no right or wrong way to hold your needles. Once you start knitting, you will soon find the most comfortable position for you. In the UK and the US, the yarn is usually held in the right hand (see step 5 on page 20), but in Europe, it is often held in the left hand (see below right). Whichever hand you use, it will control the tension of your yarn, i.e. how tightly you hold it.

HOW TO HOLD THE NEEDLES

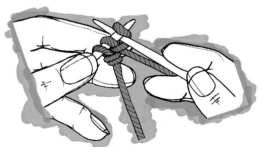

I hold my needles between my thumb and index finger.

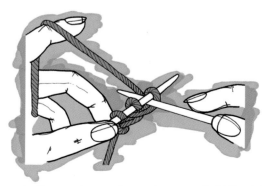

In Europe, the needles and yarn are held like this.

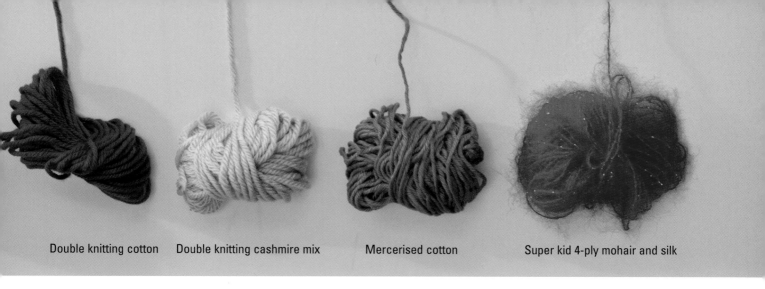

Double knitting cotton   Double knitting cashmire mix   Mercerised cotton   Super kid 4-ply mohair and silk

CHOOSING A YARN AND NEEDLES

There are so many different types of yarns on the market today and this can make it confusing to know exactly what yarn you should choose, taking into account the type of project you are making.

The three factors you should take into account when choosing a yarn are weight (or thickness), composition (what it's made of), and length.

Weight This is based on the number of plies (or strands) the yarn is made up of. The thinnest yarn is 2-ply and it goes up in size through 3-ply, 4-ply, double knit (DK), aran, and chunky to super-chunky.

Composition Yarns are made up of many different fibres, from natural ones such as merino wool, alpaca, silk, cotton and linen to man-made ones such as nylon, acrylic and viscose. The yarn's ball band will always tell you what the yarn is made of and also give you washing information.

Length The meterage of yarn in a ball can vary, even if the yarns are the same type and the balls weigh the same. It is the meterage that is vital, so if you are using a different yarn to the one in a pattern, check the ball band for the meterage and make sure you buy enough.

Like wool, needles also come in various materials – metal, plastic, bamboo and wood. All of them will give the same results, but some people prefer bamboo needles because they are lighter and can be easier to work with, while others prefer metal or plastic. At the end of the day, it's what works best for you.

Needles also come in different sizes and lengths and your choice of needle will usually be based on the weight of yarn you will be using – the ball band will give you recommendations. The length of the needle will depend on the project you are working on (i.e. if you need to cast on a large number of stitches, then choose a long pair of needles). Using chunky yarn on thick needles will mean your knitting grows quickly.

A knitting pattern will always tell you what type of yarn to use and what size of needle. If you want to choose a different yarn from that suggested, the important thing to do is to match the tension to the one given in the pattern. A suggested tension will usually be shown on the ball band.

equipment

To be honest, all you really need is a pair of needles and some yarn, but as with anything, you can buy as much or as little equipment as you like. Here are a few things that will ease your knitted life.

① **Tape measure:** this is a handy thing to have, especially when checking your tension square at the beginning of a project.

② **Knitter's sewing or darning needles:** These are essential for darning in ends and sewing up your project. If you are using a very chunky yarn, make sure that it will fit through the eye of your needle.

③ **Scissors:** A small pair of scissors is always useful for trimming ends of yarns.

④ **Knitters pins:** When you are sewing up your project, you will find these helpful in keeping the fabric in place.

⑤ **Bobbins:** When working with different colours in a project these are really handy to have. They will help keep the different yarns from tangling and speed up the process of knitting with colour.

⑥ **Notepad and pen:** This is always good to have on hand, especially if you are designing a new project, or just need to keep count of your rows and stitches when working on a project.

⑦ **Knitter's graph paper:** Good to have if you want to create your own knitted motif (see page 37).

⑧ **Stitch counter:** If you hang one on the end of each needle, it will help you keep count of what row you are on. If you have only one counter, remember to count two rows each time.

⑨ **Crochet hook:** Useful for tweaking stitches or picking up dropped ones, as well as adding a fringe to a scarf, for example.

Cable needles are used in cable knitting (see pages 38). They come in several different designs, but you will soon find out which one suits you best.

tension

You will always hear the word 'tension' in a conversation about knitting. It's the number one word in any knitter's vocabulary, but what does it mean?

Your tension is how tightly or loosely you knit. Most people don't realise how important it is to get it right until they begin their first project, but it will affect the size of your finished garment or accessory. If you knit tightly your project might end up too small or if you knit loosely it might end up too big.

Always knit a tension square before you start a project. Use the same needles, yarn and stitch pattern as the project does.

The knitting pattern you are using will tell you how many stitches and rows you should have to 10cm/4in, so cast on at least 6 more stitches than the number given and knit at least 6 more rows.

MEASURING YOUR TENSION SQUARE

Lay the square flat on a surface. To count the stitches, lay a tape measure horizontally across the square – with the end a couple of stitches in from the edge – and count the number of stitches to 10cm/4in. To count the rows, do the same thing but lay the tape vertically across the square.

If you have too few stitches, try again with larger needles. If you have too few, use smaller needles. Don't try to knit at a different tension to that which comes naturally to you; you won't be able to keep it up throughout the project.

how to cast on

This is where it all starts. Casting on is the way of getting the right number of stitches onto your needle to begin your project.

RACHEL'S TIP: When getting started, try holding your needles loosely and don't be afraid of them – if you make a mistake, remember you can always undo the yarn and start all over again.

The cable method works well with stocking stitch and the thumb method is ideal with garter stitch.

Whether you use the cable or thumb method of casting on, don't pull on the yarn too hard or your cast on will be too tight and it will be hard to knit the first row.

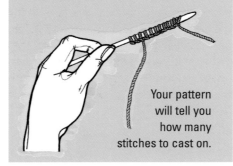

Your pattern will tell you how many stitches to cast on.

CABLE METHOD

This method of casting on gives a firm, strong edging to your knitted fabric.

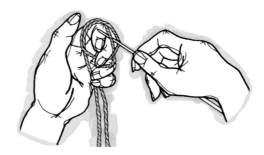

1 Before you cast on your stitches, leave a arm's short tail of yarn and make a slip knot by winding the yarn round twice around two fingers on your left hand, with the second loop behind the first one.

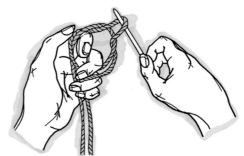

2 With a knitting needle in your right hand, pull the second loop of yarn through the first loop on your fingers.

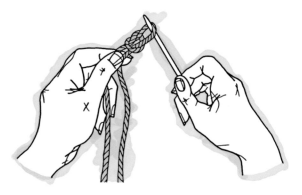

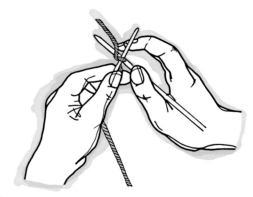

3 Pull both ends of the yarn to tighten the knot. You now have your first cast on stitch. Hold this needle in your left hand.

4 Using the right-hand needle, go through the bottom of the slip knot on the left-hand needle. Then take the main yarn around the back of the right-hand needle and between both needles.

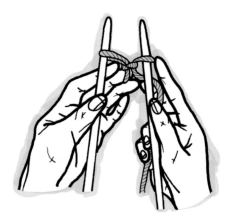

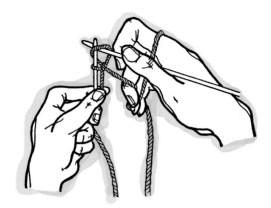

5 Slide the right-hand needle down through the the slip knot on the left-hand needle and under, pulling the yarn lying over the right-hand needle through the loop on the left-hand needle. You should now have a loop on each needle.

6 Slip the loop on the right-hand needle onto the left-hand needle and gently pull the yarn tight. You should now have 2 stitches on the left-hand needle. Working into the first stitch on the left-hand needle, repeat steps 4–6 until you have the required number of cast on stitches (see diagram in box, opposite).

THUMB METHOD

This gives you a more elastic edging to your piece of knitted fabric.

First, follow steps 1–3 of Cable Method, leaving a long yarn tail.

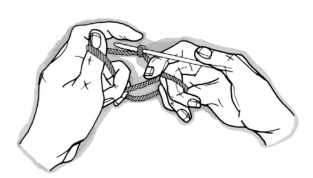

4 You are now going to use the long tail of yarn to cast on all your stitches. Take hold of the tail of yarn with three of your fingers and go over the top and under with your thumb, twisting the yarn around your thumb.

5 Slide the right-hand needle under the bottom of the thumb loop.

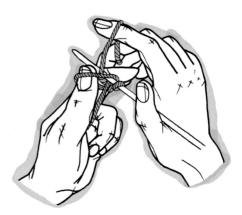

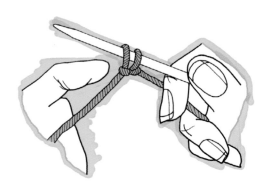

6 Take the main bit of yarn around the back of the needle and lift the thumb loop over the needle.

7 Pull the tail of yarn tight. You should now have 2 cast on stitches on your needle. Repeat steps 4–7 until you have the required number of cast on stitches on your needle.

how to knit (k)

A knit stitch is the most basic type of stitch.

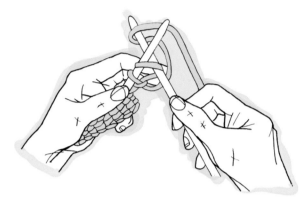

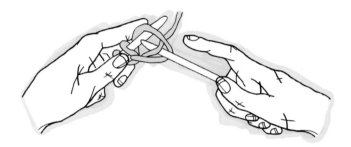

1 With the main working yarn at the back of the work, insert the right-hand needle through the bottom of the first stitch and to the back of the left-hand needle, making a cross with the needles. Take the main working yarn around the back of the right-hand needle and then between both needles.

2 Slide the right-hand needle down through the top of the loop on the left-hand needle and under, pulling the yarn lying over the right-hand needle through the loop. Pull the yarn tight.

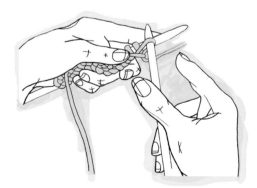

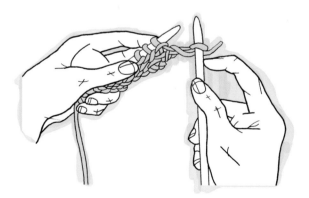

3 Slip the original stitch off the left-hand needle.

4 Repeat these steps until all the stitches on the left needle have been knitted. This is called a row.

how to purl (p)

A purl stitch is the second-most basic type of stitch and is the reverse of the knit stitch.

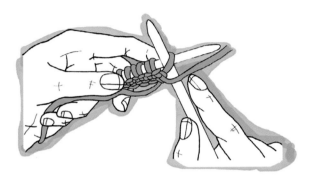

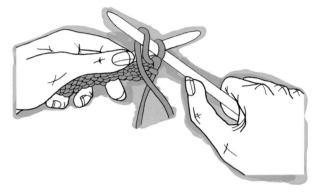

1 With the working yarn at the front of the work, insert the right-hand needle in through the top of the first stitch on the left-hand needle and to the front, making a cross with the needles.

2 Take the main working yarn around the back of the right-hand needle to the front.

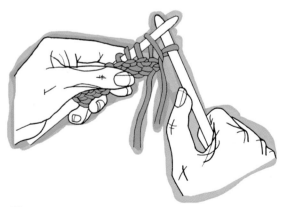

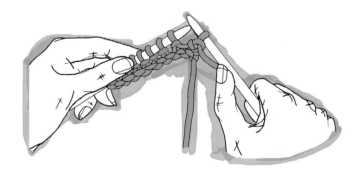

3 Slide the right-hand needle down through the bottom of the loop on the left-hand needle, pulling the yarn through the loop and pull tight.

4 Slip the original stitch off the left-hand needle. Repeat these steps until all the stitches on the left-hand needle have been purled.

how to cast off

Casting off is a very simple process and is done after you have finished your piece of knitting to secure your stitches so they don't unravel.

1 First of all, you need to knit 2 stitches.

2 Using the left-hand needle, pick up the first knitted stitch on the right-hand needle.

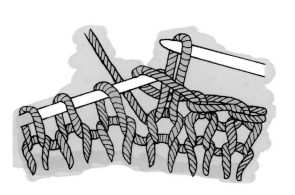

3 Carry this stitch over your second knitted stitch on the right needle and let it drop off the left needle. Knit another stitch and repeat steps 2 and 3.

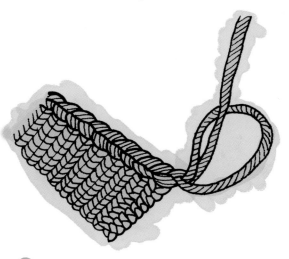

4 Once you have cast off all your stitches, pass the end of the yarn through the last stitch and pull tightly.

basic stitch patterns

By combining your two basic stitches, knit and purl, you can produce lots of simple knitted textures such as garter, stocking, moss and rib.

RACHEL'S TIP: Basic stitch patterns are so much fun to do as they don't take too much time or concentration. Why not combine two of these stitch patterns together and create your own knitted fabric design.

You can then get a bit more experimental and try combining knit and purl stitches in other patterns.

① GARTER STITCH

Garter stitch is the most basic knitted fabric and is produced by simply knitting (or purling) on every single row. This forms a strong and firm pattern of raised horizontal ridges and the knitted fabric will not curl at the edges.

To make garter stitch, cast on any number of stitches and knit every row. You can work garter stitch with every row purl, but this is rarely done.

② STOCKING STITCH

This is probably the most commonly used knitting stitch pattern. The knit stitches on stocking stitch are referred to as the right side (shown here) and the purl stitches the wrong side. The purl side is also called the reverse stocking stitch. This looks similar to a garter stitch, but the ridges are slightly smaller and closer together in reverse stocking stitch.

To make stocking stitch, cast on any number of stitches. On the first row knit all the stitches, on the second row, purl all the stitches and repeat these rows to the end.

③ MOSS STITCH

This is one of my favourite stitches. It's not the quickest of stitches as you need to keep lifting the yarn back and forth after each stitch, but it gives a nice firm piece of knitted fabric that doesn't curl at the sides. This fabric is usually created by casting on an odd number of stitches and always beginning and ending with a knit stitch.

To make moss stitch, cast on an uneven number of stitches. On the first row, knit the first stitch, purl the next and repeat to the end – you will finish on a knit stitch. Do the same for the following rows.

④ RIB STITCH

This fabric is composed of vertical 'ribs' of stitches. You can make a rib as big or as small as you want by adjusting the number of stitches you knit and purl on each row.

To make double rib stitch (shown here), cast on a multiple of 4 stitches plus 2 extra. On the first row, knit 2, then purl 2, then knit 2 and repeat to the end. On the 2nd row, begin with 2 purl stitches, then 2 knit stitches. Repeat these 2 rows to the end.

shaping

Increasing and decreasing simply mean adding or reducing the number of stitches. Use these techniques to shape your knitted project.

RACHEL'S TIP: Making a stitch 'M1' doesn't show much, so is often used if you want to increase in the middle of a row.

Increasing a stitch 'inc 1' shows more as there is a little bar of yarn across the bottom of the new stitch. It's often used on an edge, as the bar will disappear into the seam when the pieces of knitting are sewn together.

'K2tog' (shown overleaf) slants to the right on a knit row, while 'p2tog' slants to the left on a purl row. 'Skpo' slants to the left on a knit row and is often used at the other end of a row to 'k2tog' to produce mirror-image decreases.

INCREASING

Making a stitch (make one 'M1')

1 Using your left-hand needle, pick up the horizontal strand lying in between both needles.

2 Using the right-hand needle, go through the back of the picked-up strand on the left-hand needle and knit it as usual.

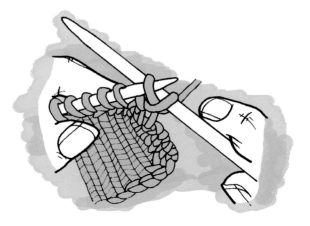

Increasing a stitch (inc 1)

1 Using your right-hand needle, go into the stitch and knit it as usual, but do not slip the original stitch off the left-hand needle.

2 Using the right-hand needle, go through the back of the same stitch and knit the stitch again.

3 Slip the original stitch off the left-hand needle.

DECREASING

Knit 2 together ('k2tog')

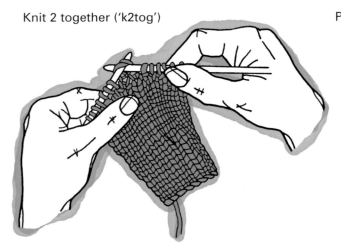

1 On a knit row, using your right-hand needle go through the bottom of next 2 stitches on your left-hand needle and to the back, and knit them together.

Purl 2 together ('p2tog')

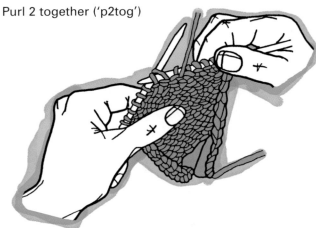

2 On a purl row, using your right-hand needle, go in through the top of the next 2 stitches on your left-hand needle and to the front, and purl them together.

Slip 1, knit 1, pass slipped stitch over ('skpo')

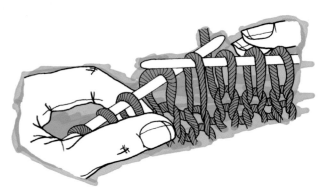

1 Using your right-hand needle, go through the bottom of the next stitch on your left-hand needle and slip it onto your right needle. Knit the next stitch.

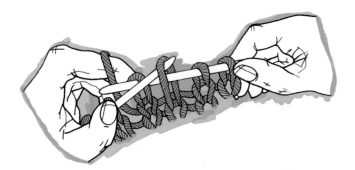

2 Using your left-hand needle, pick up the slipped stitch on your right-hand needle and pass it over your knitted stitch.

finishing

So you've got to the end of the pattern safely and you've cast off your project, but how do you put it together?

RACHEL'S TIP: Before you sew the pieces together you need to darn in any tails of yarn left from casting on and off, joining in new balls of yarn, or from colour work. Thread a darning needle with the tail and weave the needle through the backs of four or five adjacent stitches, pulling the yarn through. Then weave it back on itself to secure it. Do not pull the yarn too tight or the knitted fabric will pucker.

Take your time sewing up: you put effort into knitting the project, so don't rush now and spoil it.

BACKSTITCH

Backstitch forms a thick, strong and firm seam and is usually used with lightweight yarns. With this stitch, you are working on the wrong sides of the knitted fabric with the right sides placed together.

Using a darning needle, work 0.5cm from the edge of the knitting. Go through the centre of a stitch to match it to the same stitch on the other edge, and make each stitch about 1cm long.

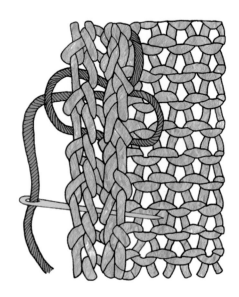

MATTRESS STITCH

Mattress stitch is my favourite way of sewing up as it creates a completely invisible seam, but it can sometimes take a little practice to get right.

With the right sides of the knitting facing you, pick up the first 2 horizontal bars between the first and the second stitches on the left piece of knitting. Now go across to the right piece and pick up the same 2 bars on that piece.

Go back across to the left piece and pick up the next 2 bars in between the stitches and then pick up the same 2 bars on the opposite piece. Continue like this, firmly pulling the yarn to form the seam.

EDGE TO EDGE STITCH

This is the best method to use when knitting with lightweight yarns.

Working with the wrong sides facing you, place both pieces of fabric together, matching them row for row and stitch for stitch. Taking the needle through the head of each stitch, sew the seam up in a zig-zag fashion, as shown below.

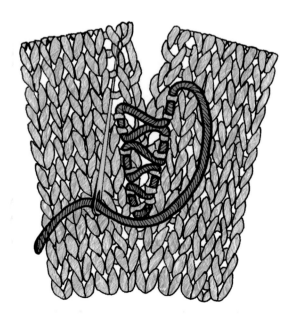

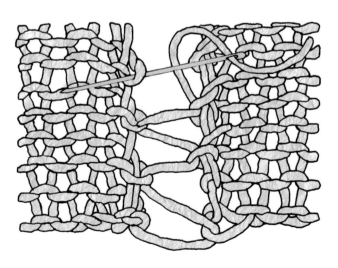

knitting with beads

This is a lovely and very simple decorative method that you can use to make knitted jewellery, purses or garments.

KNITTING WITH BEADS

Beaded knitting is one of my favourite techniques. I love the way that, just by adding beads to a plain knitted design, you can make it look really glamorous. Beading can take longer than other decorative techniques but it's always worth being patient with.

Before casting on, loop a length of thread around the yarn and thread the ends through a needle.

One at a time, slide the beads down the needle and thread and onto the yarn. The pattern will tell you how many beads to thread on, but I always thread on a few more just to be safe. Push the beads down the yarn a short way and cast on the stitches needed.

ADDING BEADS WITH A SLIP STITCH

Adding beads with a slip stitch is the most common way of beading knitting and it works on both the knit side and the purl side rows. However, you can only add a bead on every other stitch and alternate row. The steps below show how to bead on a knit row. If working a purl row, bring the yarn to the back of the work, and slip the stitch knit-wise.

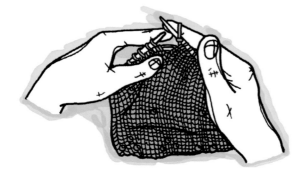

① On a knit row, push the next bead up and bring the yarn through between the needles and to the front of the work.

② Slip the next stitch purl-wise from your left-hand needle onto your right-hand needle.

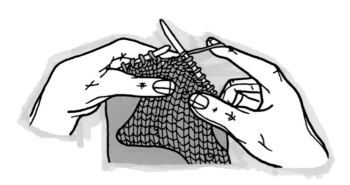

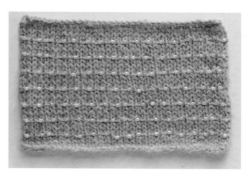

③ Bring the yarn back between the needles and to the back of the work, making sure your bead is lying at the front of the work. The bead is now in a secured position. Continue with the pattern as usual.

WORKING A SIMPLE BEADED SWATCH

Thread 119 beads onto the yarn. Cast on 35 stitches.
Row 1: Knit.
Row 2: Purl.
Repeat rows 1–2 once more.
Row 5: *Knit 1, bead 1, repeat from * to the last stitch, knit 1.
Repeat rows 2–5, 6 more times. Cast off.

basic colour work

Changing colour can sound quite intimidating, but actually the most difficult thing about it is keeping your yarns from tangling.

RACHEL'S TIP: There are two different types of colour knitting – Fair Isle and intarsia. Whichever method you use, wind as much yarn of each colour as possible onto its own bobbin and work from the bobbins. This will help prevent the yarns from tangling up.

Fair Isle is used when a colour pattern is being repeated right along a row. The yarn that is not being knitted with at any point in the pattern is woven into the back of the knitted fabric using either the weaving or stranding technique. Therefore, a Fair Isle fabric is effectively double-thickness and can be quite stiff. Be very careful not to pull the woven or stranded yarn too tight, or the fabric will bunch up on the front.

Intarsia knitting is used when you are working a large motif in a knitted fabric. Each section of colour (the motif and the background on either side) uses a separate ball of yarn. The yarns need to be looped around each other at the edges of each section to avoid holes.

JOINING YARN

1 When joining a new shade of yarn into a row of stitches, place the end of the yarn between the tips of the needles and across the main shade from left to right.

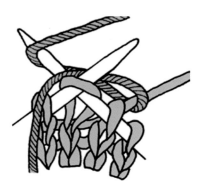

2 Take the new yarn under the main yarn and knit the next stitch with it. Move the end of the main shade off the needle as the new stitch is formed.

WEAVING IN COLOUR

Use this method if more than 4 stitches of the same shade are being worked.

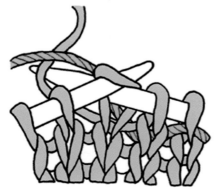

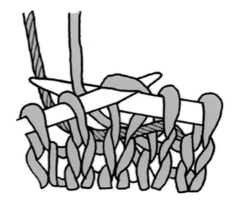

1 To weave in yarn on the right side (a knit row), insert the right-hand needle into the next stitch and lay the yarn to be woven in over the right-hand needle. Knit the stitch with the main shade of yarn, taking it under the yarn not in use.

2 Knit the next stitch with the main shade of yarn, taking it over the yarn being woven in. Continue to do this, weaving the yarn not in use over and under the main shade of yarn until you need to start working with it again.

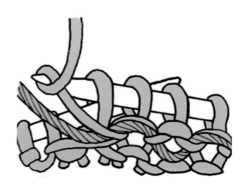

3 To weave on the wrong side (a purl row), do the same as you would do for the right side, but purl the stitch with the main shade of yarn and take it under the yarn not in use.

4 Purl the next stitch with the main shade of yarn, taking it over the yarn being woven in. Continue to do this, weaving the yarn not in use over and under the main shade of yarn until you need to start working with it again.

STRANDING COLOUR

Use this method if less than 4 stitches of the same shade are being worked.

1 On the right side (a knit row), when knitting the first stitch in a group in the main shade of yarn, insert the right-hand needle into the stitch and take the main shade over the contrast shade of yarn. Knit the main shade stitches.

2 When knitting the first stitch in a group in the contrast shade of yarn, insert the right-hand needle into the stitch and take the contrast shade under the main shade. Knit the contrast shade stitches.

3 On the wrong side (a purl row), when purling the first stitch in a group in the main shade, insert the right-hand needle into the next stitch and take the main shade over the contrast shade. Purl the main shade stitches.

4 When purling the first stitch in a group in the contrast shade, insert the right-hand needle into the next stitch and take the contrast shade under the main shade. Purl the contrast shade stitches.

5 Your knitted fabric should look nice and neat on the wrong side, where all the stranded colour will be visible (see below).

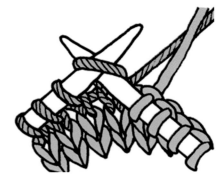

INTARSIA

Use this method to work a larger colour motif.

On the right side (a knit row), when knitting the first stitch in a new shade of yarn, insert the right-hand needle into the stitch and take the old shade over the new shade of yarn (see above). Knit all the stitches in the new shade.

On the wrong side (a purl row), when purling the first stitch in a new shade, insert the right-hand needle into the next stitch and again, take the old shade over the new shade. Purl all the stitches in the new shade.

Use these techniques every time you start working with a new shade of yarn. On the back of the knitted fabric the yarns will end up looped around each other along the colour joins, preventing unwanted holes appearing between colours.

FOLLOWING A CHART/GRAPH

When following a chart, always start with a knit row and the right-hand side of the chart. The arrows on the chart below indicate which direction to go in. So, you start at arrow number 1 and read all the odd-numbered rows from right to left and the even-numbered rows from left to right. Each represents 1 stitch and is coloured to match the yarn used.

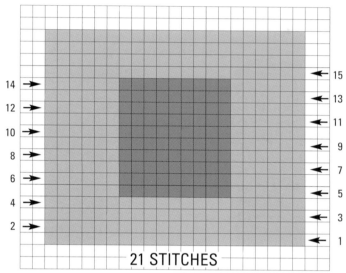

21 STITCHES

cabling

A cable is simply a group of twisted stitches, created by placing a number of stitches on a cable needle and holding them at the front or back of the work.

RACHEL'S TIP: To make them show up well, cables are usually worked in stocking stitch on a background of reverse stocking stitch. In these diagrams the stitches being cabled are shown in a darker colour so you can see what is happening more clearly.

The cables shown here are worked over 6 stitches, though this number can vary. A back cable worked over 6 stitches is abbreviated as 'C6B' and a front cable as 'C6F'. If they were worked over 4 stitches they would be 'C4B' and 'C4F'. A front cable makes the stitches twist to the left and a back cable makes them twist to the right.

CABLING TO THE FRONT

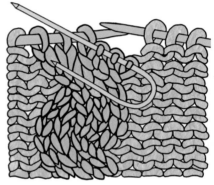

1 Knit to the position of the cable. Using a cable needle, pick up the next 3 stitches, holding the cable needle at the front of the work.

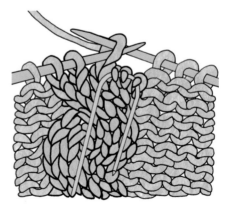

2 Now, knit the next 3 stitches on the left-hand needle, ignoring the stitches on the cable needle.

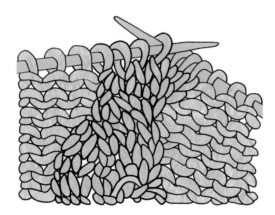

③ Slip the 3 stitches on the cable needle onto the left-hand needle and knit them.

CABLING TO THE BACK

Do the same as above, but hold the cable needle at the back of the work. You can knit the stitches straight from the cable needle if it's easier.

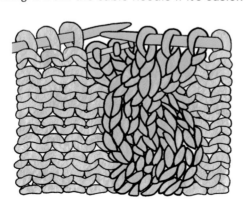

WORKING A SIMPLE CABLE SWATCH

This is an example of a basic cable pattern and it has been worked over 6 rows.

Cast on 42 stitches.
Row 1: p4, k6, p8, k6, p8, k6, p4.
Row 2: k4, p6, k8, p6, k8, p6, k4.
Row 3: As row 1.
Row 4: As row 2.
Row 5: p4, C6F, p8, C6F, p8, C6F, p4.
Row 6: As row 2.

Repeat these 6 rows 3 more times.
Cast off.

pompoms

I love making pompoms and I make them in many different sizes and yarns, even combining yarns in one pompom – perfect for when you need a break from knitting.

① Cut two pieces of card of the same diameter and cut a small round hole in the middle of each circle. Place them together and wind your yarn through the holes in the middle of the two pieces of card and around the outer circles.

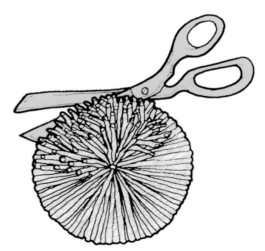

② Repeat until you have the required amount of yarn wound around both circles. Then, using a pair of scissors, cut the yarn between both circles of card so that the loops are cut open.

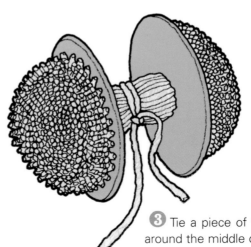

③ Tie a piece of yarn tightly around the middle of the pom-pom and remove the card. Use the yarn to attach the pompom.

felting

Felting is a really fun technique that will hide any flaws in your knitting, as well as creating a funky decorative finish.

Felting occurs when a woollen item is washed at a hot temperature in the washing machine. This results in the item shrinking and becoming thicker. The fibres bind together to make felted wool, which you can then cut into as it won't fray or unravel. This is because as the washing machine tumbles the knitting around, the agitation causes the wool to rub together and 'knit' itself tighter.

This is a great technique for beginners as any flaws or holes in the knitting tend to close up and disappear because of the shrinkage. It is also great if you don't want to spend a lot of time knitting a project or if you want to be a little bit more experimental.

The types of yarn that are most suitable for felting are those made of 100 per cent wool. The more wool your yarn contains and the higher the temperature, the better your knitted fabric will felt.

TO FELT

Just put the knitted pieces into the machine and wash them at a hot temperature. It's that easy! I always put mine in a pillowcase as it helps to agitate the fabric and help the felting. Or you could throw in an old pair of jeans or a towel. Once you have felted your knitting and left it to dry thoroughly, you can cut out your required pattern.

abbreviations

Although knitting patterns can look like a jumble of letters, you will soon become familiar with these abbreviations.

approx	Approximately
beg	Beginning
C6B	Cable 6 back
C6F	Cable 6 front
cont	Continue
DK	Double knitting
dec	Decrease
inc	Increase
k	Knit
k2tog	Knit two stitches together
k2tbl	Knit two stitches together by going through the back of both stitches.
MB	Make bobble
M1	Make a stitch
p	Purl
psso	Pass slipped stitch over
RS	Right side
Sl 1	Slip 1 stitch
sl 1, k1, skpo	Slip 1 stitch, knit 1 stitch, pass slipped stitch over
st (s)	Stitch(es)
st st	Stocking stitch
tbl	Through back of loop(s)
turn	Swap needles so work faces the opposite way
WS	Wrong side
YF	Yarn forward
YO	Yarn over
YRN	Yarn round needle

KNITTING TERMS

Asterisks and square brackets
These are used to show where a piece of work is to be repeated. For example if a pattern says to k1, *p1, k1* 3 times, you will repeat the p1, k1 in between the asterisks 3 times in total. Similarly, you repeat instructions within square brackets the stated number of times.

Stitches at the end of a row
Sometimes in a pattern, you will see a number of stitches shown in brackets, e.g. (16 stitches) at the end of a row. This is a useful marker so you can check that you have the right number of stitches on your needle.

Charts and graphs
These are used to show colour pattern instead of written instructions. Each square on the graph resembles a stitch (see page 37).

Flower Corsage (p48)

Bow-tie Necklace (p74)

Record Bag (p77)

Silk Evening Scarf (p66)

Guy's Scarf (p73),
Girl's Casual Scarf (p47)

accessories for guys & girls

To get you started, here are some projects that you can knit for yourself — scarves, bags and some beaded jewellery.

girl's casual scarf

I designed this piece on the train to Fife to visit my parents, huddled up in the corner of the carriage with my cable pin and some chunky wool. Cabling is a great way to be experimental with knitting and it's so easy to do.

MATERIALS 4 x 100g balls of Rowan Big Wool Fusion.

NEEDLES 1 pair of 15mm (US 19) needles. Cable needle.

TENSION 7 stitches and 10 rows to 10cm/4in square over stocking stitch.

ABBREVIATIONS

Cable 6 front: Slip next 3 stitches onto a cable needle and hold at front of work, knit 3 stitches from left-hand needle, then knit 3 from cable needle.

Cable 6 back: Slip next 3 stitches onto a cable needle and hold at back of work, knit 3 stitches from left-hand needle, then knit 3 from cable needle (see page 38).

PATTERN

Cast on 28 stitches.
Row 1: Knit to end of row.
Row 2: Purl to end of row.

Row 3: Knit 2, [cable 6 front, knit 2] twice, cable 6 front, knit 4 .
Row 4: Purl to end of row.
Row 5: Knit 4, [cable 6 back, knit 2] twice, cable 6 back, knit 2.
Repeat rows 2–5 until 3 balls have been knitted. Cast off.

TO MAKE UP

Use fourth ball of yarn to make a fringe for the ends of the scarf. Cut 36cm/14in lengths of yarn and loop them through the cast on and cast off stitches.

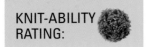

flower corsage

I love knitting flowers and I started knitting this one on a bus ride to Aberdeen to visit friends and then finished it on the way back. This would look lovely pinned on to a suit jacket or even as an accessory for a handbag.

MATERIALS 1 x 50g ball of RYC Soft Tweed in each of two shades A and B. Shirring elastic.

NEEDLES 1 pair of 6mm (US 10) needles.

TENSION 12 stitches and 16 rows to 10cm/4in square over stocking stitch

ABBREVIATIONS

M1: Make 1 stitch by picking up the strand between the stitch on the right-hand needle and the stitch on the left-hand needle and placing it on the left-hand needle, then knit into the back of it (see page 26).

K2tbl: Knit the next 2 stitches together by going through the back of both stitches.

PATTERN

Main part
Using A, cast on 8 stitches.
Row 1: Knit to end of row.
Row 2: Knit to end of row.
Row 3: Knit 1, M1 and knit to end of row.
Row 4: Knit to end of row.
Row 5: Knit 1, M1 and knit to end of row.
Rows 6, 7 and 8: Knit to end to row.
Row 9: K2tbl, knit to end of row.
Row 10: Knit to end of row.
Row 11: As row 9.
Row 12: Knit to end of row.
Row 13: Cast off 4 stitches, knit to end of row. (4 stitches).
Row 14: Knit to end of row.
Row 15: Cast on 4 stitches, knit to end of row.
Repeat rows 2–15, 9 more times, then repeat rows 2–14 again.
Cast off.

Middle of flower

Using B, cast on 5 stitches.

Row 1: Knit to end of row.

Row 2: Purl to end of row.

Row 3: Knit 1, M1, knit 3, M1, knit 1. (7 stitches).

Row 4: Purl to end of row.

Row 5: Knit 2 stitches together, knit 3, knit 2 stitches together. (5 stitches).

Row 6: Purl to end of row.

Row 7: Knit to end of row.

Row 8: Knit 2 stitches together.

Cast off.

TO MAKE UP

Thread shirring elastic through the straight edge of the main part, then pull tightly to form a rosette shape. Sew the middle into the centre of corsage.

#1 EXTREME KNITTING

Knitting at the top of Arthur's Seat, Edinburgh

THINGS TO DO WITH YOUR KNITTING NEEDLES:

#1 USE THEM AS COCKTAIL STIRRERS

muff

Knit this simple design to look cool among your friends and keep your fingers nice 'n' cosy in the freezing winter weather.

MATERIALS 1 x 100g ball of Rowan Big Wool in each of 2 shades A and B.

NEEDLES 1 pair of 10mm (US 15) needles.

TENSION 10 stitches and 13 rows to 10cm/4in square over stocking stitch.

ABBREVIATIONS

Loop 1 (a loop stitch): Knit the next stitch, but do not take stitch off left-hand needle, take the yarn forward between the needles, pass yarn round left thumb and then to back of work between the needles, knit into the same stitch again and remove from left-hand needle. Wind yarn over right-hand needle once, then pass the 2 stitches over this stitch, knit next stitch.

Note: Carry yarn that is not in use up the side of the work, twist yarns neatly on every alternate row.

PATTERN

Using A, cast on 23 stitches.
Row 1: Knit to end of row.
Row 2: Purl to end of row.
Row 3: Knit 1, *Loop 1, knit 1*, repeat from * to end of row.
Row 4: Purl to end.
Rows 5–24: Repeat rows 1–4, 5 more times.
Rows 25–28: Using B, purl to end of row.
Rows 29–32: Using A, purl to end of row.
Rows 33–36: Using B, purl to end of row.
Rows 37–40: Using A, purl to end of row.
Using A, cast off.

TO MAKE UP

Sew up using mattress stitch (see page 31) by joining cast on and cast off edge together.
Make strap by plaiting 3 strands of B together.
Sew ends to edge of seam.

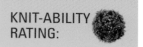
stripey hat & gloves

Loud, bright and very warm, I designed this matching set to cheer myself up over winter and then to top them off, I added bows to the fingerless gloves. I love bows because I always think they look great as a feature on a knitted design and they are really simple to make.

For the hat

MATERIALS 1 x 100g ball of Rowan Big Wool in each of two shades A and B.

NEEDLES 1 pair of 10mm (US 15) needles.

TENSION 10 stitches and 13 rows to 10cm/4in square over stocking stitch.

Note: Carry yarn that is not in use up the side of the work, twist yarns neatly on every alternate row.

PATTERN

Using A, cast on 40 stitches.
Row 1: Knit 1, *purl 2, knit 2, repeat from* to last 3 stitches, purl 2, knit 1.
Row 2: Purl 1, *knit 2, purl 2, repeat from * to last 3 stitches, knit 2, purl 1.
Rows 3–6: Repeat rows 1–2 twice more.

Row 7: Using B, knit to end of row.
Row 8: Using B, purl to end of row.
Row 9: Using A, knit to end of row.
Row 10: Using A, purl to end of row.
Rows 11–16: Repeat rows 7–10 once more, then rows 7–8.
Row 17: Using A, [knit 7, Knit 3 stitches together] 4 times.
Row 18: Using A, purl to end of row.
Row 19: Using B, [knit 5, Knit 3 stitches together] 4 times.
Row 20: Using B, purl to end of row.
Row 21: Using A, [knit 3, knit 3 stitches together] 4 times.
Row 22: Using A, [purl 2 stitches together] 8 times. Cast off.

Break yarn and thread through remaining stitches. Pull up tight and fasten off securely.

TO MAKE UP

Join seam using mattress stitch (see page 31).

For the gloves

MATERIALS   1 x 100g ball of Rowan Big Wool in each of two shades A and B.

NEEDLES   1 pair of 10mm (US 15) needles.

TENSION   10 stitches and 13 rows to 10cm/4in square over stocking stitch.

ABBREVIATIONS

Turn: Swap needles, so work faces the other way.

PATTERN

Left hand
Using A, cast on 20 stitches.
Row 1: Knit 1, *purl 2, knit 2, repeat from * to last 3 stitches, purl 2, knit 1.
Row 2: Purl 1, *knit 2, purl 2, repeat from * to last 3 stitches, knit 2, purl 1.
Rows 3–6: Repeat rows 1 and 2 twice more.
Row 7: Using A, knit to end of row.
Row 8: Using A, purl to end.
Row 9: Using B, knit to end.
Row 10: Using B, purl to end of row.
Rows 11–14: Repeat rows 7–10.
Rows 15–16: Repeat rows 7–8.
Row 17 (make bow): Using B, knit 12, turn, cast on 12 stitches, turn, knit to end of row. (32 stitches).
Row 18: Using B, purl to end.
Rows 19–20: Repeat rows 7–8.
Row 21 (make thumb hole): Using B, knit 4, bring yarn forward and over needle, knit 2 stitches together, knit to end.

Row 22: Using B, purl to end of row.
Row 23: Using A, knit 12, cast off 12, knit to end.
Row 24: Using A, purl to end of row.
Rows 25–26: Repeat rows 9–10.
Cast off.

Right hand
Using A, cast on 20 stitches.
Row 1: Knit 1, *purl 2, knit 2, repeat from * to last 3 stitches, knit 1.
Row 2: Purl 1, *knit 2, purl 2, repeat from * to last 3 stitches, knit 2, purl 1.
Rows 3–6: Repeat rows 1–2 twice more.
Row 7: Using A, knit to end of row.
Row 8: Using A, purl to end of row.
Row 9: Using B, knit to end of row.
Row 10: Using B, purl to end of row.
Rows 11–14: Repeat rows 7–10.
Rows 15–16: Repeat rows 7–8.
Row 17 (make bow): Using B, knit 8, turn, cast on 12 stitches, turn, knit to end of row. (32 stitches).
Row 18: Using B, purl to end of row.
Rows 19 to 20: Repeat rows 7–8.
Row 21 (make thumbhole): Using B, knit 14, knit 2 stitches together. bring yarn forward and over needle, knit to end of row.
Row 22: Using B, purl to end.
Row 23: Using A, knit 12, cast off 12, knit to end.
Row 24: Using A, purl to end.
Rows 25–26: Repeat rows 9–10.
Cast off

TO MAKE UP

Sew sides together using mattress stitch (see page 31). Using A, sew up the gap underneath the bow from the inside, carry yarn around centre of bow and pull tight to create bow shape.

THINGS TO DO WITH YOUR WOOL: #1 USE IT AS A WASHING LINE

small handbag

I love using Ribbon Twist, it's one of my favourite yarns and always looks good when knitted up. This wee handbag would be great for taking on a night out, a perfect size for your money, phone and makeup.

MATERIALS   2 x 100g balls of Rowan Ribbon Twist.
4 Rowan buttons.

NEEDLES   1 pair of 12mm (US 17) needles.
Cable needle.

TENSION   9 stitches and 13 rows to 10cm/4in square over stocking stitch.

ABBREVIATIONS

Cable 10 back: Slip the next 5 stitches onto a cable needle and hold at back of work, knit 5 stitches from left-hand needle, then knit 5 from cable needle (see page 38).

Yarn forward: Bring yarn forward between the needles, then take it over the right-hand needle to make 1 stitch.

PATTERN

Main part
Cast on 28 stitches.
Row 1: Knit to end of row.
Row 2: Purl to end of row.
Row 3: Knit to end of row.
Row 4: Purl to end of row.
Row 5: Knit 2, cable 10 back, knit 4, cable 10 back, knit 2.
Row 6: Purl to end of row.
Rows 7–38: Repeat rows 1–6, 5 more times, then rows 1 and 2 again.
Cast off

Gusset (make 2)
Cast on 5 stitches.
Row 1: Knit to end of row.
Row 2: Purl to end of row.
Rows 3–18: Repeat rows 1–2, 8 more times.
Cast off.

Handles (make 2)
Cast on 6 stitches.
Row 1: Knit to end of row.
Row 2: Purl to end of row.
Row 3 (buttonhole row): Knit 3, yarn forward, knit 2 together, knit 1.
Row 4: Purl to end of row.
Rows 5 to 42: Repeat rows 1–2, 19 more times.
Row 43 (buttonhole row): Knit 3, yarn forward, knit 2 together, knit 1.

Row 44: Purl to end of row.
Rows 45–46: As rows 1–2.
Cast off.

TO MAKE UP

With centre of cast on edge of gussets to centre of side of main part, sew gussets in place using mattress stitch (see page 31). Sew on buttons. Button handles in place.

THINGS TO DO WITH YOUR KNITTING NEEDLES:

#2 USE THEM TO LABEL YOUR HOUSE PLANTS!

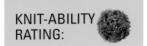

two-colour scarf

This was one of the first designs I did for this book. It looks more difficult to do than it actually is and is just a matter of increasing and decreasing. I began it at my first knitting circle and the following week it was complete!

MATERIALS 1 x 50g ball of Rowan Kid Classic in each of 2 shades A and B.

NEEDLES 1 pair of 5.5mm (US 9) needles.

TENSION 18 stitches and 23 rows to 10cm/4in square over stocking stitch.

ABBREVIATIONS

Turn: Swap needles, so work faces the other way.

Note: Carry yarn not in use up the side of the work, twist yarns neatly on every alternate row.

PATTERN

Using A, cast on 18 stitches.

Rows 1–6: Knit to end of row.
Row 7: Cast off 14 stitches, knit to end of row.
Row 8: Change to B, knit 4, turn and cast on 14 stitches.
Rows 9–14: Knit to end of row.
Row 15: Cast off 14 stitches, knit to end of row.
Row 16: Change to A, knit 4, turn and cast on 14 stitches.
Repeat rows 1–16, 25 more times.
Repeat rows 1–6.
Cast off all stitches.

fluffy shawl

I created this on Christmas day with festive spirit. The brushed wool looks enchanting and you could wear this to a party or to keep cosy in the evening.

MATERIALS 5 x 100g balls of Rowan Biggy Print. 1.5m/60in ribbon.

NEEDLES 1 pair of 10mm (US 15) needles.

TENSION 9 stitches and 11 rows to 10cm/4in square over stocking stitch.

ABBREVIATIONS

Loop 1 (a loop stitch): Knit the next stitch, but do not take stitch off left-hand needle, yarn forward between the needles, pass yarn round left thumb and then to back of work between the needles, knit into the same stitch again and remove from needle. Wind yarn over needle once, then pass the 2 stitches over this stitch.

PATTERN

(Make 2 pieces)

Cast on 20 stitches.

Row 1: Purl 1, *knit 1, purl 1, repeat from * to last stitch, knit 1.
Row 2: Knit 1, *purl 1, knit 1, repeat from * to last stitch, purl 1.
Row 3: Purl 1, *knit 1, purl 1, repeat from * to last stitch, knit 1.
Row 4: Knit 1, *purl 1, knit 1, repeat from * to last stitch, purl 1.
Row 5: Purl 1, * loop 1, repeat from * to last stitch, knit 1.
Row 6: Knit 1, *purl 1, knit 1, repeat from * to last stitch, purl 1.
Rows 7–30: Repeat rows 1–6, 4 more times.
Cast off.

TO MAKE UP

Join the two panels together using back stitch or mattress stitch. Cut each loop and tie in a knot, brush out each strand to create brushed out fluffy effect. Cut ribbon in half and sew one piece to each front.

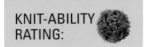
silk evening scarf

Kid Silk Haze is a really delicate yarn, so I designed a scarf you could wear as an everyday accessory or on a night out. You will need to use double thickness here, so wind the yarn into two equal-sized balls before you begin.

MATERIALS 1 x 25g ball of Rowan Kid Silk Haze Night. Wind into 2 balls.

NEEDLES 1 pair of 5mm (US 8) needles.

TENSION 25 stitches and 34 rows to 10cm/4in square over stocking stitch.

ABBREVIATIONS

M1: Make 1 stitch by picking up the strand between the stitch on the right-hand needle and the stitch on the left-hand needle and placing it on the left-hand needle, then knit into the back of it (see page 26).

PATTERN

Cast on 8 stitches.
Row 1: Knit to end of row.
Row 2: Knit to end of row.
Row 3: Knit 1, M1, knit to end of row.
Row 4: Knit to end of row.
Row 5: Knit 1, M1, knit to end of row.
Rows 6, 7 and 8: Knit to end of row.
Row 9: Knit 2 together through the back of the stitches, knit to end of row.
Row 10: Knit to end of row.
Row 11: Knit 2 together through the back of the stitches, knit to end of row.
Row 12: Knit to end of row.
Row 13: Cast off 4 stitches, knit to end of row.
Row 14: Knit 4.
Row 15: Cast on 4 stitches, knit these 4 stitches, knit to end.
Repeat rows 2–15 until there is enough yarn left to cast off, ending with a row 13. Cast off.

bumpy bag

I'm forever losing my wool and needles around my flat. This bag is the perfect solution and will keep all your knitting stuff together – just pick it up and take it travelling, to the pub or to your knitting circle.

MATERIALS 4 x 100g balls of Rowan Biggy Print. 1 x 100g ball of Rowan Spray – wind into 2 balls.

NEEDLES 1 pair of 15mm (US 19) needles.

TENSION 7 stitches and 10 rows to 10cm/4in square over stocking stitch.

ABBREVIATIONS

MB (make bobble): (knit 1, purl 1, knit 1, purl 1, knit 1) all into next stitch, turn needles and purl 5 stitches, turn needles and knit 5 stitches, turn needles and purl 2 stitches together, purl 1, purl 2 stitches together, turn needles, knit 3 stitches together.

Turn: Swap needles, so work faces the other way.

PATTERN

(Make 2 pieces)
Using Biggy Print, cast on 11 stitches.

Row 1: Knit to end of row.
Row 2: Purl to end of row.
Row 3: Knit 1, *MB, knit 1, repeat from * to end.
Row 4: Purl to end of row.
Rows 5–10: Repeat rows 1–2, 3 more times.

Repeat rows 1–10, 2 more times.
Break off Biggy Print.

Join in 2 ends of Spray and use double thickness.

Next row: Knit 1, [purl 2, knit 2] twice, purl 2.
Next row: Knit 2, [purl 2, knit 2] twice, purl 1.
Repeat the last 2 rows once more.
Cast off

Gusset (make 2)
Using Biggy Print, cast on 5 stitches.

Row 1: Knit to end of row.
Row 2: Purl to end of row.
Repeat these 2 rows until gusset fits from centre of cast on edge of main part to beginning of rib section of back and front, ending with a row 2. Break off Biggy Print.

Join on two ends of Spray and use double thickness.

Next row: Knit 1, purl 2, knit 2.
Next row: Purl 2, knit 2, purl 1.

Repeat the last 2 rows once more.
Cast off.

Handle (make 2)
Using two ends of Spray, cast on 6 stitches.

Row 1: Knit 1, purl 2, knit 2, purl 1.
Rows 2–18: Repeat row 1, 17 times.
Cast off.

TO MAKE UP

Join cast on edges of gusset pieces. With gusset seam to centre of cast on edge of main part sew gussets in place. Sew on handles.

THINGS TO DO WITH YOUR KNITTING NEEDLES:

#3 USE THEM AS CHOPSTICKS!

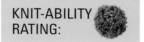
guy's chunky scarf

I designed this in order to inspire a guy to knit it, but it would be a great scarf for a girl as well. The diagonal stripes make it look harder than it is, but the technique is really simple and it will just take you an evening to do.

MATERIALS 2 x 100g balls of Rowan Biggy Print in each of 2 shades A and B.

NEEDLES 1 pair of 20mm (US 36) needles.

TENSION 7 stitches and 10 rows over 10cm/4in square over stocking stitch.

Note: Carry yarn not in use up the side of the work, twist yarns neatly on every alternate row.

ABBREVIATIONS

M1: Make 1 stitch by picking up the strand between the stitch on the right-hand needle and the stitch on the left-hand needle and placing it on the left-hand needle, then knit into the back of it (see page 26).

PATTERN

Using A, cast on 12 stitches.
Row 1: Knit 2 together, knit to end of row.
Row 2: Knit 1, M1, knit to end of row.
Row 3: Knit 2 together, knit to end of row.
Row 4: Knit 1, M1, knit to end of row.

Change to B.
Rows 5–8: Using B, work as rows 1–4.
Repeat rows 1–8, 8 more times.
Using B cast off.

bow-tie necklace

I designed this while my friends were relaxing on the couch with some wine on a lazy Friday evening. As I beaded away, they drank away and after a couple of bottles of wine my necklace was complete!

MATERIAL
1 x 50g ball of Rowan Kid Classic. 3 packets of Jaeger beads (about 400 beads).

NEEDLES
1 pair of 5.5mm (US 9) needles.

TENSION
18 stitches and 23 rows to 10cm/4in square over stocking stitch.

ABBREVIATIONS

Bead 1 (B1): Bring yarn to front of work between the needles, slide 1 bead up close to work, slip next stitch, take yarn to back of work (see page 32).

PATTERN

Thread on 297 of your chosen beads before casting on.
Each bead row requires 9 beads.

Cast on 19 stitches.
Row 1: Knit to end of row.
Row 2: Knit 1, purl to last stitch, knit 1.
Row 3: Knit 1, *bead 1, knit 1, repeat from * to end.
Row 4: Knit 1, purl to last stitch, knit 1.
Row 5: Knit to end of row.
Row 6: Knit 1, purl to last stitch, knit 1.
Repeat rows 1–6, 32 more times.
Cast off.

TO MAKE UP

Press the knitted fabric. Tie the long piece of beaded fabric into a bow, securing with some Kid Classic.

Make a chain by threading on 100 beads onto a length of Kid Classic and sew each end to the top of the bow (see photograph).

record bag

My brother came up with this idea, as he wanted a bag he could carry around. You can use it to carry records, or your purse or wallet, phone and mobile. When working from the chart, use the intarsia method (see page 36)

MATERIALS   3 x 50g balls of Rowan Handknit Cotton DK in main colour (M). 1 x ball in contrast colour (C). 30cm/12in zip.

NEEDLES   1 pair of 4mm (US 6) needles.

TENSION   20 stitches and 28 rows to 10cm/4in square over stocking stitch.

PATTERN

Back and front (make 2)
Using M, cast on 8 stitches
Work circle in stocking stitch, following the chart on the following page, shaping sides by increasing, casting on, decreasing or casting off, as required (see overleaf). Cast off.

Handle
Cast on 16 stitches.
Continue in stocking stitch until handle measures 150cm/60ins.
Cast off.

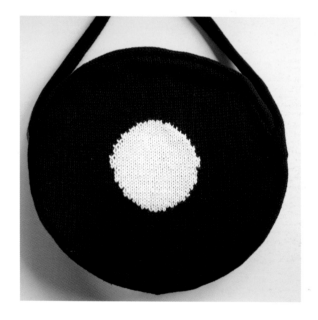

Zip placket (make 2)
Cast on 10 stitches.
Continue in stocking stitch until placket measures 50cm/20ins.
Cast off.

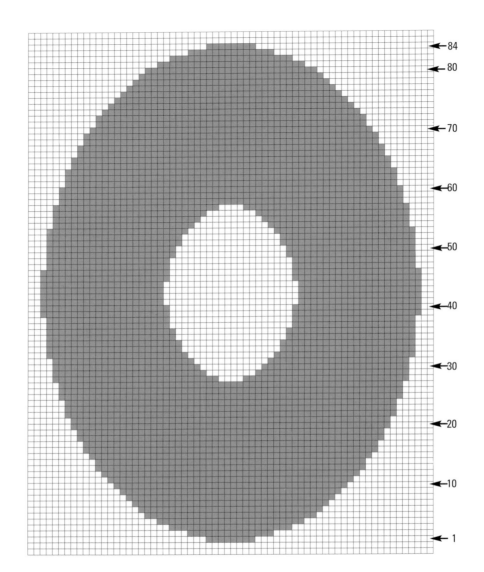

84 ←
80 ←
70 ←
60 ←
50 ←
40 ←
30 ←
20 ←
10 ←
1 ←

TO MAKE UP

Using mattress stitch, join placket pieces together for 15cm/6in at each end, leaving 30cm/12in open at centre. Sew in zip. Join cast on and cast off edges of handle together. Leaving 50cm/20in free, sew handle between back and front to form gusset join at centre of cast on edges. Sew zip placket in place, tucking ends in behind handle.

CHART

See page 37 for instructions for following a chart.

To increase a single stitch, use Inc1 (see page 27) on the edges of the knitting. To increase several stitches, cast them on. To decrease a single stitch, use k2tog or p2tog (see page 28). To decrease several stitches, cast them off.

Glasses Case (p100)

Slippers (p82)

Laptop Case (p87)

Place Mats (p96)

Tea Cosy (p91)

knitting for an occasion

Once you have gained more confidence, you can make gifts for your friends – something that you can style to suit their tastes and personality.

slippers

Last Christmas I bought my flatmate a pair of red chunky slippers, this year I thought I'd knit her a pair instead. These are really easy to do as I've just used stocking stitch, and they are really quick to knit up.

MATERIALS
4 x 100g balls of Rowan Biggy Print.

NEEDLES
1 pair of 15mm (US 19) needles.

TENSION
7 stitches and 10 rows to 10cm/4in square over stocking stitch.

ABBREVIATIONS

M1: Make 1 stitch by picking up the strand between the stitch on the right-hand needle and the stitch on the left-hand needle and placing it on the left-hand needle, then knit into the back of it (see page 26).

PATTERN

Front (make 2)
Cast on 9 stitches.

Row 1: Knit to end of row.
Row 2: Purl to end of row.
Row 3: Slip 1, knit 1, pass slipped stitch over stitch just knitted, knit 5, knit 2 stitches together.
Row 4: Purl to end of row.
Row 5: Slip 1, knit 1, pass slipped stitch over stitch just knitted, knit 3, knit 2 stitches together.
Row 6: Purl to end of row.
Row 7: Slip 1, knit 1, pass slipped stitch over stitch just knitted, knit 1, knit 2 stitches together.
Row 8: Purl 3 together and fasten off.

Left side (make 2)
Cast on 13 stitches.

Row 1: Knit to end of row.
Row 2: Purl to end of row.
Row 3: Knit 1, M1, knit to end of row. (14 stitches).
Row 4: Purl to end of row.
Row 5: Knit 1, M1, knit to end of row. (15 stitches).
Row 6: Purl to end of row.
Row 7: Knit 1, M1, knit to end of row. (16 stitches).
Row 8: Purl to end of row.
Row 9: [Slip 1, knit 1, pass slipped stitch over stitch just knitted] twice, knit to end of row. (14 stitches).
Row 10: Purl to end of row.
Row 11: [Slip 1, knit 1, pass slipped stitch over stitch just knitted] twice, knit to end. (12 stitches).
Row 12: Purl to end of row.
Row 13: [Slip 1, knit 1, pass slipped stitch over stitch just knitted] twice, knit to end. (10 stitches).
Row 14: Purl to end of row.
Row 15: [Slip 1, knit 1, pass slipped stitch over stitch just knitted] twice, knit to end. (8 stitches). Cast off.

Right side (make 2)

Cast on 13 stitches.

Row 1: Knit to end of row.
Row 2: Purl to end of row.
Row 3: Knit to last stitch, M1, k1. (14 stitches).
Row 4: Purl to end of row.
Row 5: Knit to last stitch, M1, k1. (15 stitches).
Row 6: Purl to end of row.
Row 7: Knit to last stitch, M1, k1. (16 stitches).
Row 8: Purl to end of row.
Row 9: Knit to last 4 stitches, [knit 2 stitches together] twice. (14 stitches).
Row 10: Purl to end of row.
Row 11: Knit to last 4 stitches, [knit 2 stitches together] twice. (12 stitches).
Row 12: Purl to end of row.
Row 13: Knit to last 4 stitches, [knit 2 stitches together] twice. (10 stitches).
Row 14: Purl to end of row.
Row 15: Knit to last 4 stitches, [knit 2 stitches together] twice. (8 stitches).
Cast off.

Sole (make 2)

Cast on 5 stitches.

Row 1: Knit to end of row.
Row 2: Purl to end of row.
Row 3: Knit 1, M1, knit to last stitch, M1, knit 1 (7 stitches).
Row 4: Purl to end of row.
Row 5: Knit 1, M1, knit to last stitch, M1, knit 1 (9 stitches).
Row 6: Purl to end of row.
Rows 7 to 14: Work in stocking stitch.
Row 15: Slip 1, knit 1, pass slipped stitch over stitch just knitted, knit to last 2 stitches, knit 2 stitches together. (7 stitches).
Row 16: Purl to end of row.
Row 17: Slip 1, knit 1, pass slipped stitch over stitch just knitted, knit to last 2 stitches, knit 2 stitches together. (5 stitches).

Row 18: Purl to end of row.
Cast off.

TO MAKE UP

Sew up using mattress stitch (see page 31), but instead of working on the right sides, work on the wrong sides to create a visible seam. Join left and right side from cast off edge to 'point'. Then sew row ends of front to remaining row ends of left and right sides, then join to sole.

POMPOMS

Use two 5cm diameter circles of card and the remaining yarn make two pompoms (see page 40). Attach to slippers by darning in the binding yarn around the ankle of the slipper, so that you can pull tight to tighten slipper.

#3 EXTREME KNITTING

Lovely ladies knitting in Nigeria.

laptop case

Even a laptop needs some beauty sleep in the hustle and bustle of everyday life, so wrap it up in this bobbly cover and give it the rest it deserves – a perfect graduation gift.

MATERIALS

1 x 100g ball of Rowan Biggy Print in Shade A.
2 x balls in Shade B.
4 x buttons.

NEEDLES

1 pair of 12mm (US 17) needles.

TENSION

8 stitches and 11 rows to 10cm/4in square over stocking stitch.

ABBREVIATIONS

MB (make bobble): (knit 1, purl 1, knit 1, purl 1, knit 1) all into next stitch, turn needles and purl 5 stitches, turn needles and knit 5 stitches, turn needles and purl 2 stitches together, purl 1, purl 2 stitches together, turn needles, knit 3 stitches together.

Turn: Swap needles, so work faces the other way.

YO (yarn over): take yarn over the needle to make 1 stitch.

Note: Carry yarn that is not in use up the side of the work, twist yarns neatly on every alternate row.

PATTERN

Main piece

Using B, cast on 20 stitches.

Row 1: Knit 1, *purl 2, knit 2, repeat from * to last 3 stitches, purl 2, knit 1.
Row 2: Purl 1, *knit 2, purl 2, repeat from * to last 3 stitches, knit 2, purl 1.
Row 3: Knit 1, [purl 2, YO, knit 2 stitches together] 4 times, purl 2, knit 1.
Row 4: Purl 1, *knit 2, purl 2, repeat from * to last 3 stitches, knit 2, purl 1.
Row 5: Knit 1, *purl 2, knit 2, repeat from * to last 3 stitches, purl 2, knit 1.
Row 6: Purl 1, *knit 2, purl 2, repeat from * to last 3 stitches, knit 2, purl 1.

Change to A.
Row 7: Knit to end of row.
Row 8: Purl to end of row.
(These 2 rows form stocking stitch.)

Rows 9–40: Work in stocking stitch.
Row 41: *Knit 4, MB, repeat from * to last 5 stitches, knit to end of row.

Row 42: Purl to end of row.

Row 43: Knit to end of row.

Row 44: Purl to end of row.

Row 45: Knit 2, *MB, knit 4, repeat from * to last 5 stitches, MB, knit 2.

Row 46: Purl to end of row.

Row 47: Knit to end of row.

Row 48: Purl to end of row.

Rows 49–56: Repeat rows 41–48 once more.

Rows 57–60: Repeat rows 41–44 once more.

Rows 61–62: Using B, work in stocking stitch.

Rows 63–64: Using A, work in stocking stitch.

Rows 65–66: Using B, work in stocking stitch.

Rows 67–70: Using A, work in stocking stitch.

Rows 71–74: Using B, work in stocking stitch.

Rows 75–76: Using A, work in stocking stitch.

Cast off.

Gussets (make 2)

Using A, cast on 4 stitches.

Row 1: Knit to end of row.

Row 2: Purl to end of row.

(These 2 rows form stocking stitch.)

Rows 3–32: Work in stocking stitch.

Cast off.

TO MAKE UP

Sew buttons onto row 72. Using mattress stitch, (see page 31), sew gussets to each side of cover, between cast off edge and beginning of stocking stitch. Fold over rib part and fasten to buttons.

THINGS TO DO WITH YOUR WOOL:
#3 MAKE A CAT'S CRADLE

tea cosy

I originally saw this idea in a knitting catalogue from the 1940s and wanted to come up with my own design that was a bit more modern. A perfect gift for your mum on Mother's Day!

MATERIALS   1 x 50g ball of Rowan Calmer in each of two shades A and B.

NEEDLES   1 pair of 5mm (US 8) needles.

TENSION   21 stitches and 30 rows to 10cm/4in square over stocking stitch.

Note: When carrying yarn across back of stitches pull slightly tight to form 'pucker' and twist each shade after every 4th stitch. Always twist both yarns at the beginning of the row.

PATTERN

Make 2 pieces.

Using A, cast on 80 stitches.
Row 1: *Using A, knit 10, using B, knit 10, repeat from * to end of row.
Row 2: *Using B, purl 10, using A, purl 10, repeat from * to end of row.

Rows 3–10: Repeat rows 1–2, 4 times.
Row 11: *Using B, knit 10, using A, knit 10, repeat from * to end of row.
Row 12: *Using A, purl 10, using B, purl 10, repeat from * to end of row.
Rows 13–20: Repeat rows 11–12, 4 times.
Rows 21–30: Repeat rows 1–2, 5 times.
Rows 31–36: Repeat rows 11–12, 3 times.
Row 37: *Using B, knit 1, knit 2 stitches together through the back of the stitches, knit 5, knit 2 stitches together. Using A, k1, knit 2 stitches together through the back of the stitches, knit 5, knit 2 together, repeat from * to end of row. (64 stitches).
Row 38: * Using A, purl 1, purl 2 stitches together through the back of the stitches, purl 3, purl 2 stitches together, using B, purl 1, purl 2 stitches together through the back of the stitches, purl 3, purl 2 together, repeat from * to end of row. (48 stitches).
Row 39: * Using B, knit 1, knit 2 stitches together through the back of the stitches, knit 1,

knit 2 stitches together. Using A, knit 1, knit 2 stitches together through the back of the stitches, knit 1, knit 2 stitches together, repeat from * to end of row of row. (32 stitches).

Row 40: *Using A, [purl 2 stitches together] twice, using B [purl 2 stitches together] twice, repeat from * to end of row. (16 stitches).

Cast off.

TO MAKE UP

Join side seams together using mattress stitch, leaving holes for spout and handle. Run a gathering thread through cast off edge and pull up tightly. Secure ends.

POMPOM

Using A, make a large pompom (see page 40), and attach to top of cosy.

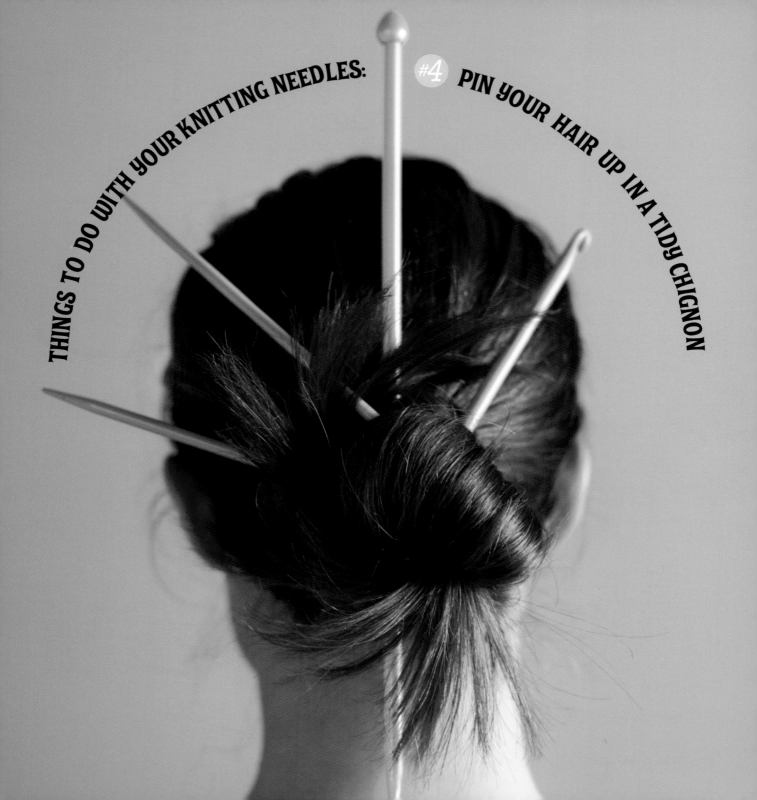

THINGS TO DO WITH YOUR KNITTING NEEDLES: **#4** PIN YOUR HAIR UP IN A TIDY CHIGNON

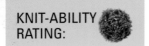

wine-bottle top

I saw this idea in an old knitting magazine and thought it would be great to give with a bottle of champagne or wine for an engagement party. The simple rib in this design makes it quick to knit up and the glitter in the wool provides a glamorous look.

#4 EXTREME KNITTING

Knitting on a camel...
sure to be a bumpy ride,
so watch those stitches!

MATERIALS 1 x 50g ball of RYC Soft Lux.

NEEDLES 1 pair of 5mm (US 8) needles.

TENSION 18 stitches and 24 rows to 10cm/4in square over stocking stitch.

PATTERN

Cast on 50 stitches.

Row 1: Knit 1, *purl 4, knit 4* to last stitch, purl 1. Repeat row 1, 28 more times.

Cast off.

TO MAKE UP

Join side seam using mattress stitch (see page 31). Make two small pompoms (see page 40). Using the central binding yarn, attach to top of side seam.

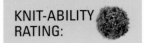
place mats

These are always a good thing to have around during parties and would make an ideal house-warming present, especially if your mates have just bought new tables!

MATERIALS 1 x 50g ball of Rowan Handknit Cotton DK in each of 3 shades A, B and C will make approx 24 circular or triangular mats in various stripes.

NEEDLES 1 pair of 4.5mm (US 7) needles.

TENSION 20 stitches and 28 rows to 10cm/4in square over stocking stitch.

ABBREVIATIONS

M1: Make 1 stitch by picking up the strand between the stitch on the right-hand needle and the stitch on the left-hand needle and placing it on the left-hand needle, then knit into the back of it (see page 26).

PATTERN

Circular mats
Using A cast on 12 stitches.
Row 1: Knit to end of row.
Row 2: Purl to end of row.
(These 2 rows form stocking stitch.)
Row 3: Knit 1, M1, knit 10, M1, knit 1. (14 stitches).
Row 4: Purl to end of row.
Row 5: Knit 1, M1, knit 12, M1, knit 1. (16 stitches).
Row 6: Purl to end of row.

Join in B.
Row 7: Knit 1, M1, knit 14, M1, knit 1. (18 stitches).
Rows 8–12: Work in stocking stitch.

Join in C.
Row 13: Knit 1, M1, knit 16, M1, knit 1. (20 stitches).
Row 14–16: Work in stocking stitch.
Row 17: Knit 2 stitches together through the back of the stitches, knit to the last 2 stitches, knit 2 stitches together. (18 stitches)
Row 18: Purl to end of row.

Join in B.

Row 19: Knit 2 stitches together through the back of the stitches, knit to the last 2 stitches, knit 2 stitches together. (16 stitches).

Row 20: Purl to end of row.

Row 21: Knit 2 stitches together through the back of the stitches, knit to the last 2 stitches, knit 2 stitches together. (14 stitches).

Row 22: Purl to end of row.

Row 23: Knit 2 stitches together through the back of the stitches, knit to the last 2 stitches, knit 2 stitches together. (12 stitches).

Row 24: Purl to end of row.

Cast off.

Triangular mats

Using A, cast on 5 stitches.

Row 1: Knit 1, M1, knit 3, M1, knit 1. (7 stitches).
Row 2: Purl to end of row.
Row 3: Knit 1, M1, knit 5, M1, knit 1. (9 stitches).
Row 4: Purl to end of row.
Row 5: Knit 1, M1, knit 7, M1, knit 1. (11 stitches).
Row 6: Purl to end of row.

Join in B.

Row 7: Knit 1, M1, knit 9, M1, knit 1. (13 stitches.)
Row 8: Purl to end of row.
Row 9: Knit 1, M1, knit 11, M1, knit 1. (15 stitches).
Row 10: Purl to end of row.
Row 11: Knit 1, M1, knit 13, M1, knit 1.
(17 stitches).
Row 12: Purl to end of row.

Join in C.

Row 13: Knit 1, M1, knit 15, M1, knit 1. (19 stitches).
Row 14: Purl to end of row.
Row 15: Knit 1, M1, knit 17, M1, knit 1. (21 stitches).
Row 16: Purl to end of row.
Row 17: Knit 1, M1, knit 19, M1, knit 1. (23 stitches).
Row 18: Purl to end of row.

Join in B.

Row 19: Knit 1, M1, knit 21, M1, knit 1. (25 stitches).
Row 20: Purl to end of row.
Row 21: Knit 1, M1, knit 23, M1, knit 1. (27 stitches).
Row 22: Purl to end of row.
Row 23: Knit 1, M1, knit 25, M1, knit 1. (29 stitches).
Row 24: Purl to end of row.
Cast off.

THINGS TO DO WITH YOUR WOOL

#4 GIFT-WRAP PRESENTS WITH IT!

glasses case

I felted this project to make it a bit sturdier – this case will hold either sunglasses or spectacles and you can even make some felted letters, for example a name, to sew onto the front of the case.

MATERIALS 1 x 100g ball of Rowan Big Wool Fusion.
1 x 50g ball of RYC Soft Tweed.

NEEDLES 1 pair of 10mm (US 15) needles.

TENSION 10 stitches and 13 rows to 10cm/4in square over stocking stitch using Big Wool fusion.

ABBREVIATIONS

MB (make bobble): (Knit 1, purl 1, knit 1) all into next stitch, turn needles and purl 3 stitches together, turn needles.

Turn: Swap needles, so work faces the other way.

PATTERN

Using Big Wool Fusion, cast on 23 stitches
Row 1: Knit to end of row.
Row 2: Purl to end of row.
(These 2 rows form stocking stitch.)
Rows 3 and 4: Work in stocking stitch.
Row 5: Knit 1, *MB, knit 1, repeat from * to end of row.
Rows 6–8: Work in stocking stitch.

Row 9: Knit 2, *MB, knit 1, repeat from * to last stitch, knit 1.
Rows 10–12: Work in stocking stitch.
Rows 13–20: As rows 5–12.
Cast off

TO ADD LETTERS

Using RYC Soft Tweed, cast on 20 stitches.
Row 1: Knit to end of row.
Row 2: Purl to end of row.
(These 2 rows form stocking stitch.)
Work a further 16 rows in stocking stitch.
Cast off.

To felt, put the pieces in separate pillow cases and machine wash at 60 degrees.

Leave to dry.

TO MAKE UP

Join side seams using mattress stitch.
Cut out your chosen letters and sew onto case using a matching colour of thread.
Make handle by plaiting 3 stands of Big Wool Fusion to measure 35cm. Sew one end to top of each side seam.

dice

When my best friend passed her driving test, I knitted her a pair of quirky woolly dice. Felting is so much fun to do and when you experiment with it, you can come up with some really interesting and fun designs.

MATERIALS 1 x 100g ball of Rowan Big Wool in each of two shades A and B.
Matching thread.
Toy wadding (for stuffing).

NEEDLES 1 pair of 12mm (US 17) needles.

TENSION 8 stitches and 11 rows to 10cm/4in square over stocking stitch.

PATTERN

(Knit 1 piece from each ball.)
Cast on 20 stitches.
Continue in stocking stitch to end of ball, leaving enough yarn to cast off.
Cast off.

To felt, put the pieces in separate pillow cases and machine wash at 60 degrees.
Once felted, leave to dry, then cut out 12 8x8cm squares and 42 circles of each colour.

TO MAKE UP

Sew circles on sides of dice with some matching thread. Sew squares together to form a cube, but before sewing the last side one, stuff the cube.

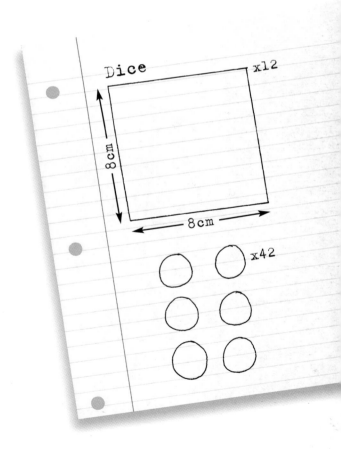

Louise's Knitted Cuff
(p110)

Amy's Corsage (p106)

Kate's Painted Bag (p118)

Suzie's Evening Bag
(p114)

customising designs

At my knitting clubs I'm always looking for new inspiration or ways to inspire others. Customising has become very popular recently in knitwear as more and more people become experimental and use this craft as an outlet for their creativity. So, I decided to brief five people who have either a textile, design or fashion background to create a design using their particular skill as an inspiration, whether in customising a basic knitted design or using a particular method of knitting.

In this chapter you will see that there are lots of ways of experimenting with this craft even if you are just a beginner, so please feel free to improvise and use your own skill and passion in your designs.

Di's Lacy Pants
(p122)

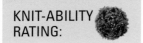
Amy's corsage

This is a funky corsage that reminds me of the 1920s, when everything was so elegant and sexy.

MATERIALS 1 x 25g ball of Rowan Yorkshire Tweed 4 ply. Wind into 2 balls.
1 x 50g ball of Rowan Lurex Shimmer.

NEEDLES 1 pair of 4.5mm (US 7) needles.

TENSION 26 stitches and 38 rows to 10cm/4in square over stocking stitch using Yorkshire Tween yarn used in double thickness.

PATTERN

Using Yorkshire Tweed double, cast on 50 stitches.
Row 1: Knit to end of row.
Row 2: Purl to end of row.
Repeat the last 2 rows until there is enough yarn left to cast off.
Cast off.

TO MAKE UP

Put the piece of knitted fabric in the washing machine on a 60 degree wash (add detergent and an old towel to help agitate the knitting).
Reshape and dry flat.

Draw two different-sized petal-shaped templates and cut out five petals of each size. Pinching the larger ones at the bottom end, sew them together to create a flower shape. Add the smaller petals behind the larger ones in the gaps.

Add a circular piece of felt over the centre of the flower to hide any stitching. Add further decoration if you like.

Once all petals have been sewn together use some Rowan Lurex Shimmer and embroider around each petal and add black ribbon to the back to create a rosette impression. Sew on a hairpin or brooch pin.

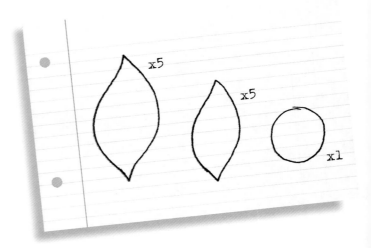

felted fun

The idea behind this design was to create something that was structured and three-dimensional.

NAME: Amy Gooda

AGE: 25

BACKGROUND: Constructed Textile Design, Gray's School of Art, Aberdeen.

MY STORY

I have always enjoyed creating structures and decorative forms and during my time at university I tried many different approaches to creating three-dimensional pieces. Since graduating I have spent a lot of time using my knitting machine to create fabric that has a three-dimensional element to it. Felting is something that I am still learning about as there are so many different techniques and finishes which can be achieved. At the moment I am still creating ideas and samples, trying various different approaches to see what works best for me.

MY INSPIRATION

I chose to create a felted flower because it meant I could create layers and make a structured form. This is much easier to do with felted pieces and I wanted to stick with a smaller project as you can see the results more quickly, ideal if this is your first attempt at felting. Also, because the piece is felted, it is much more robust and less likely to fall apart. It's also easier to customise – by adding some shimmering yarn and ribbon, you can make something very simple look fabulously sophisticated. Corsages are really versatile, you can pin it in your hair or on your clothes or bag.

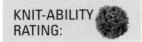
Louise's knitted cuff

This is a really simple design, but you can make the trimming as elaborate as you like – or design it to complement your own style.

MATERIALS
1 x100g ball of Rowan Big Wool in each of two shades.
12 Rowan buttons in different colours.
3 packets of Jaeger beads (in different colours).

NEEDLES
1 pair of 10mm (US 15) needles.

TENSION
10 stitches and 13 rows to 10cm/4in square over stocking stitch.

PATTERN

Cast on 20 stitches.
Work 16 rows in garter stitch (knitting every row), changing colour as you wish.

TO MAKE UP

Sew 2 rows of 3 buttons on one short edge of the knitted piece to fasten the cuff together – just push the buttons through the knitting on the opposite edge.

Once the cuff is complete, customise the design using more buttons and add beads to join the button design.

#5 EXTREME KNITTING

Knitting on a hill top...
Let your surroundings
inspire you.

beaded jewels

I design wire-knitted jewellery, but here I chose to emphasise the knitted aspect and used buttons and beads as decoration.

NAME: Louise Pringle

AGE: 29

BACKGROUND: Constructed Textile Design, Heriot-Watt University.

MY STORY

A couple of years after I graduated from Heriot–Watt after studying Textile Design I showed a friend the work I had done for my degree show. I had made six final garments which incorporated knitted and beaded jewellery with wire at the neck and wrist areas which I then graduated into the actual garment. It crossed the boundaries of clothing and jewellery. My friend took the garments into work and came back with 10 orders for knitted jewellery and wire cuffs. I now design different types of jewellery, which I sell in around 23 retailers, mostly in Scotland (www.eclecticshock.net).

MY INSPIRATION

I liked the idea of making an accessory that could be fastened to fit around any part of the arm, or even the ankle. In order for this to work it had to be adjustable. Thick wool knitted with big needles meant there were natural gaps in the knitting, big enough for average-sized buttons to be pushed through. I attached two rows of buttons on the edge of the knitted piece, which enabled the piece to be buttoned quite tightly around relatively large parts of the limb.

Suzie's evening bag

This is a really simple pattern, but the addition of the embroidery makes it stand out. You can sew your own design freehand, or trace the template overleaf, or use any other pattern you like.

MATERIALS
3 x 50g balls of RYC Cashsoft DK.
1 x 25g ball of Rowan Kidsilk Haze.
1 x 50g ball of Rowan Lurex Shimmer.
1 x 50g ball of Rowan Handknit Cotton DK.
1 pair of bamboo handles.
2 metal poppers.
Embroidery needles.

NEEDLES
1 pair of 4.5mm (US 7) needles.

TENSION
22 stitches and 30 rows to 10cm/4in square over stocking stitch using Cashsoft DK.

PATTERN

Back and front (both alike)
Using Cashsoft DK, cast on 30 stitches
Row 1: Knit to end of row.
Row 2: Purl to end of row.
Rows 3–50: Repeat rows 1–2, 20 more times.
Cast off.

Gusset
Using Cashsoft DK, cast on 4 stitches.
Row 1: Purl to end of row.

Row 2: Knit 1, M1, knit to last stitch, M1, knit 1.
Row 3: Purl to end of row.
Row 4: Knit 2, M1, knit to last 2 stitches, M1, knit 2.
Rows 5–10: Repeat rows 3–4, 3 more times. (14 stitches).
Row 11: Purl to end of row.
Row 12: Knit to end of row.
Row 13: Purl to end of row.
Rows 14–79: Repeat rows 11–12, 33 more times.
Row 80: Knit 2, slip 1 stitch, pass slipped stitch over, knit to last 4 stitches, knit 2 stitches together, knit 2.
Row 81: Purl to end of row.
Rows 82–87: Repeat rows 80–81, 3 more times.
Row 88: Knit 1, slip 1 stitch, pass slipped stitch over, knit 2 stitches together, knit 1.
Row 89: Purl to end of row.
Cast off.

TO MAKE UP

Sew cast on and cast off edge of front and back to left and right side of gusset using mattress stitch. Embroider flower and leaf design using Kidsilk Haze, lurex shimmer and Rowan Handknit Cotton DK.

Once the bag is finished, attach 2 bamboo handles to the side seams.

printed textile

Here, I've taken the concept of printing on textiles and transferred it to knitting and embroidery.

NAME: Suzie McGill

AGE: 25

BACKGROUND: Printed Textile Design, Edinburgh Art College, Heriot-Watt University.

MY STORY

I studied printed textile design where I regularly printed on various fabrics and wools. Embroidery is also important to me and is something I use a lot in my design work now. I've been interested in knitting ever since I began experimenting with different wools at art college and found that when I merged wool and print together I could come up with some different and unique designs. Knitting is a very relaxing and rewarding activity where you can create your own fabric to work onto: there are endless possibilities for experimenting.

MY INSPIRATION

My inspiration comes from nature, especially flowers, where ideas can be taken from the many colours, textures and shapes.

Suzie's flower and leaf design

Kate's painted bag

The sky's the limit – once you get the hang of charts, you can create your own design and knit your own cityscape onto this bag.

MATERIALS 3 x 50g balls of Rowan Handknit Cotton DK in main colour (M). 2 x balls in a contrasting colour (C). 1 x 100g ball of Rowan Big Wool.

NEEDLES 1 pair each of size 4mm (US 6) and 10mm (US 15) needles.

TENSION 20 stitches and 28 rows to 10cm/4in square over stocking stitch using 4mm (US 6) needles and Handknit Cotton DK.

PATTERN

Back
Using M and 4mm (US 6) needles, cast on 57 stitches
Row 1: Knit to end of row.
Row 2: Purl to end of row.
Rows 3–100: Repeat rows 1–2, 49 more times.
Cast off.

Front
Using M and 4mm (US 6) needles, cast on 57 stitches.
Work in pattern from chart (right).
Cast off.

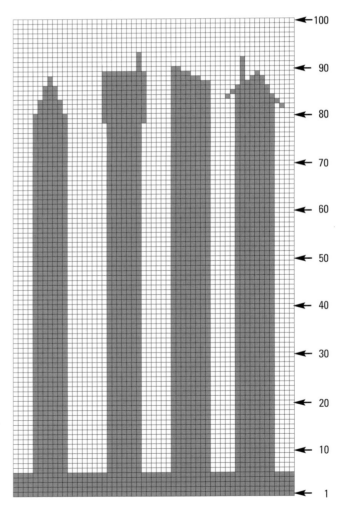

Handles (make 2)
Using 10mm (US 15) needles and Rowan Big Wool, cast on 10 stitches.
Row 1: Knit to end of row.
Row 2: Purl to end of row.
Rows 3–38: Repeat rows 1–2, 18 more times. Cast off.

TO MAKE UP

Embroider windows and lamp post onto front (see diagrams below). Join side seams. Sew on handles.

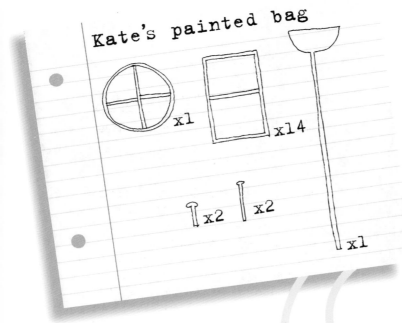

Kate's painted bag

x1 x14 x2 x2 x1

paint 'n' knit

Here I used one of my own paintings (far right) as inspiration for my knitted design.

NAME: Kate Green

AGE: 25

BACKGROUND:
Design Futures, Napier University.

MY STORY

Colour has always been a major part of my life, it gives me confidence and I use it to express my mood. I started painting with bright colours at college where I was encouraged to be more free and expressive, experimenting with shapes and different media. I then went on to do a degree in Design Futures where I got out of the habit of painting, concentrating more on graphics and computer-aided design. After university I travelled through Eastern Europe, North Africa and Australia and it wasn't until I returned to Scotland that I got back into painting. I think a part of me is rebelling against computers and the

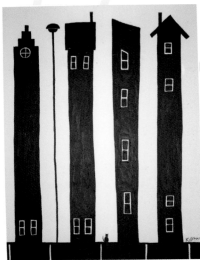

modern age, as when you are painting you are not relying on any sort of technology, you have more freedom to express your mood and each painting is original and unique.

MY INSPIRATION

I am inspired by Scotland – its small coastal villages, the Highlands and particularly Edinburgh's Old Town with its towering tenements, narrow alleyways and crowded buildings. I am also inspired by contrasting colour patterns which I feel is reflected in my artwork. I like to knit in my spare time and my paintings inspire the colours of wool I use, which is why I decided to use one of my paintings as a design for a bag. (www.kategreenartist.co.uk)

Di's lacy pants

I lined the pants with silk and added some frilly lace elastic – you could also add crazy amounts of ribbon and lace for a girly, pretty feel.

MATERIALS 2 x 50g balls of Rowan Kid Classic.

NEEDLES 1 pair of 4.5mm (US 7) needles.

TENSION 20 stitches and 25 rows to 10cm/4in square over stocking stitch.

ABBREVIATIONS

M1: Make 1 stitch by picking up the strand between the stitch on the right-hand needle and the stitch on the left-hand needle and placing it on the left-hand needle, then knit into the back of it.

YF: Bring yarn forward between needles, then take it over the right-hand needle to make 1 stitch.

PATTERN

Front
Cast on 16 stitches.
Row 1: Knit to end of row.
Row 2: Purl twice in first stitch, purl to last stitch, purl twice in last stitch. (18 stitches).
Row 3: Knit to end of row.
Rows 4 and 5: As rows 2 and 3. (20 stitches).
Row 6: Purl twice in first stitch, purl to last stitch, purl twice in last stitch. (22 stitches).
Row 7: Knit twice in first stitch, knit to last stitch, knit twice in last stitch. (24 stitches).
Rows 8–10: Repeat rows 6 and 7 once more, then row 6 again. (30 stitches).
** Row 11: Cast on 5 stitches, knit to end of row.
Row 12: Cast on 5 stitches, purl to end. (40 stitches).
Row 13: Knit 1, *knit 2 stitches together, YF, knit 1, repeat from * to last 3 stitches, knit 3.
Row 14: Cast on 3 stitches, purl to end of row.
Row 15: Cast on 3 stitches, knit to end. (46 stitches).
Row 16: Cast on 6 stitches, purl to end of row.
Row 17: Cast on 6 stitches, knit 6, *knit 2 stitches together, YF, knit 1, repeat from * to last stitch, knit 1. (58 stitches).
Row 18: Cast on 5 stitches, purl to end of row.
Row 19: Cast on 5 stitches, knit to end. (68 stitches).
Row 20: Cast on 7 stitches, purl to end of row.
Row 21: Cast on 7 stitches, knit 8, *knit 2 stitches together, YF, knit 1, repeat from * to last 2 stitches, knit 2. (82 stitches).
Row 22: Purl to end of row.
Row 23: Knit to end of row.
Row 24: Purl to end of row.
Row 25: Knit 1, *knit 2 stitches together, YF, knit 1, repeat from * to last 3 stitches, knit 3.
Row 26: Purl 2 stitches together, purl to last 2 stitches, purl 2 stitches together. (80 stitches).
Row 27: Knit to end of row.
Row 28: Purl 2 stitches together, purl to last 2 stitches, purl 2 stitches together. (78 stitches).

Rows 29–44: Repeat rows 25–28, 4 more times. On each repetition of row 25, work the lace repeat to the last 1, 2, or 3 stitches as appropriate, then knit these last stitches. (62 stitches).

Row 45: *Knit 1, purl 1, repeat from * to end of row.

Rows 46–48: Repeat row 45, 3 more times. Cast off.

Back

Cast on 30 stitches.
Purl 1 row.
Work as given for Front from ** to end.

Gusset

Cast on 30 stitches.

Row 1: Knit to end of row.

Row 2: Knit to end of row.

Row 3: Purl to end of row.

Row 4: Knit 1, slip 1, knit 1, pass slipped stitch over last knitted stitch, knit to last 3 stitches, knit 2 stitches together, knit 1.

Row 5: As row 3.

Rows 6–21: Repeat rows 4–5, 8 more times. (12 stitches).

Repeat rows 2–3 twice more.

Row 26: Knit 1, M1, knit to last stitch, M1, knit 1. (14 stitches).

Repeat row 3, then rows 2–3.

Row 30: As row 26. (16 stitches).

Row 31: Purl to end of row.

Row 32: Knit to end of row.

Row 33: Knit to end of row.
Cast off.

TO MAKE UP

Using mattress stitch, join cast on and cast off edges of gusset to cast on edges of front and back (be careful to sew through cast on and off gusset stitches, above knitted ridge). Join side seams using mattress stitch.

lacy knitwear

Why pants? Because I think knitting is so feminine and the lacy pants really express this.

NAME: Diana Kiernander

AGE: 28

BACKGROUND:
MA Fashion, London College of Fashion.

MY STORY

I'm a writer and fashion stylist really, but I enjoy knitting as it's the perfect way to relax and keep busy at the same time! Since I started knitting I've experimented greatly! Knitted nightdresses, men's jackets, puffball skirts and now the pants. Wool is wonderful for anyone with imagination. Once you've mastered the basics I honestly don't think there's anything that can't be knitted! I knit a lot in cafés and it's interesting to watch people's reaction. You get a few funny looks, but most people want to chat. They reminisce about knitting or tell you about their dog! I think knitting must be comforting to watch. No one feels threatened by a knitter, that's for sure.

MY INSPIRATION

I believe fashion is a fantasy and this feeling influences all of my work. At the same time, people who don't follow fashion but have instead their own style impress me. Strong, independent women who are super-feminine inspire my work. And I like to recall the past in my work – I think this design is certainly nostalgic. The idea of knitted pants is a little bizarre but there's a femininity about them, through the lace detail, that makes them appealing. I didn't expect anyone to want to wear these pants at first but there's been a lot of interest. Maybe because it's so cold in the winter here! Though I reckon they'd look good in summer, too, maybe worn as a bikini. You'd certainly stand out on the beach! (www.elfieloves.com)

index

acknowledgements

This book has been the best thing I've ever worked on. I've loved every minute of it and I'm so grateful I was given the opportunity by Kyle Cathie to do such a project with a team of such creative and enthusiastic people who have made this book complete and were also a pleasure to work with: my editor, Muna Reyal; my book designer, Jenny Semple; my photographer, Kate Whitaker; my models Amy Redmond, Jenny and Laura Wheatley and Jacob Love; my pattern writer Penny Hill; my illustrator, Roberta Boyce; my knitters Reinhilde Van Den Brande and my mum; as well as my friends who contributed designs to my book: Kate, Diana, Louise, Suzie and Amy, not forgetting Rowan Yarns for all their gorgeous yarn!

I would also like to thank the many inspirational and talented people whom I've met over the past few years, as well as those who currently surround me in my knitted world, without whom I would not be so inspired and driven: Sharon Brant, Debbie Abrahams, Kate Buller, Jeanette Trottman, Carol Meldrum, fellow students at Lauder College, Gray's School of Art, all the pub knitters at Sofis and, most of all, my family.

Thank you and happy knitting!

Rachel x

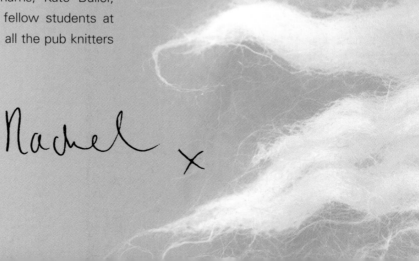